THE DISCOURSE OF THE
SYNCOPE

MERIDIAN

Crossing Aesthetics

Werner Hamacher

Editor

Translated by Saul Anton

*Stanford
University
Press*

———

*Stanford
California
2008*

THE DISCOURSE OF
THE SYNCOPE

Logodaedalus

Jean-Luc Nancy

Stanford University Press
Stanford, California

English translation © 2008 by the Board of Trustees
of the Leland Stanford Junior University. All rights reserved.

Assistance for the translation was provided by the French Ministry of Culture.

The Discourse of the Syncope: Logodaedalus was originally published in French
in 1976 under the title *Le Discours de la syncope: 1. Logodaedalus*
© 1976, Flammarion.

Printed in the United States of America on acid-free, archival-quality paper.

Library of Congress Cataloging-in-Publication Data

Nancy, Jean-Luc.
[Discours de la Syncope. English]
The Discourse of the Syncope : logodaedalus / Jean-Luc Nancy ;
translated by Saul Anton.
p.   cm.—(Meridan, crossing aesthetics)
Includes bibliographical references.
ISBN 978-0-8047-5353-1 (cloth : alk. paper)
ISBN 978-0-8047-5354-8 (pbk. : alk. paper)
1. Philosophy.   2. Style (Philosophy)   3. Kant, Immanuel, 1724–1804.
I. Title.
B53.N2513 2008
193—dc22
2007038048

Contents

Acknowledgments

Kant is in some way the hero of this book. The reader will find here a selection of documents pertaining to several episodes related to his destiny that are generally not well known. Some of these have been collected here thanks to the contributions of the following people:

Bernard Baas
Christian Bernard
Eva Brückner-Pfaffenberger
Rodolphe Gasché
Dominique Goffette
Daniel Joubert
Sarah Kofman
Philippe Lacoue-Labarthe
Allan Reiss
Jean-Michel Rey
Jean-Luc Schuster
Liliane Weissberg

Abbreviations

The following abbreviations have been used in the text for frequently cited works.

A   *Anthropology from a Practical Point of View*, trans. and ed. Robert B. Louden (Cambridge: Cambridge University Press, 2006)

C   *Correspondance*, ed. Arnulf Zweig (Cambridge: Cambridge University Press, 1999)

CJ   *Critique of Judgment*, trans. Werner S. Pluhar (Indianapolis: Hackett Publishing, 1987)

CPR   *Critique of Pure Reason*, trans. Werner S. Pluhar (Indianapolis: Hackett Publishing, 1996)

NF   *Notes and Fragments*, ed. Paul Guyer, trans. Curtis Bowman, Paul Guyer, and Frederick Hauscher (Cambridge: Cambridge University Press, 2005)

The following texts are cited from the collective volume *Practical Philosophy*, trans. and ed. Mary J. Gregor (Cambridge: Cambridge University Press, 1996):

CprR   *Critique of Practical Reason*

GW   *The Groundwork of the Metaphysics of Morals*

MM *The Metaphysics of Morals*

The following texts are cited from the collective volume *Religion and Rational Theology*, trans. and ed. Allen Wood (Cambridge: Cambridge University Press, 1996):

CF *The Conflict of the Faculties*

R *Religion Within the Boundaries of Mere Reason*

The following texts are cited from the collective volume *Theoretical Philosophy After 1781*, eds. Henry Allison and Peter Heath; trans. Gary Hatfield (Cambridge: Cambridge University Press, 2002):

PFM *Prologomena to any Future Metaphysics that Will Be Able to Come Forward as Science*

Translator's Introduction: Kant in Stereo

"Methode ist Umweg."

—Walter Benjamin

It is a truism that every text presents a translator with its own specific set of technical problems. This is certainly the case for Jean-Luc Nancy's 1976 study of Kant *The Discourse of the Syncope: Logodaedalus*. However, before considering some of its specific difficulties, it is perhaps necessary to state at the outset that these do not arise only from the usual and inevitable disjunctions between two languages and two idioms. The reasons for this are both historical and theoretical.

In the first place, *Logodaedalus* was written more than three decades ago, before much of what has since become known as "French theory"—to which the present work both does and does not belong in a very specific manner—had either been written or translated into English.[1] As a result, this translation may translate not only Nancy's original text, but also, on some level, something of "French theory." As his polemical Preamble suggests, *Logodaedalus* questions the recourse to many of the concepts and formulas that came to represent deconstructive thought in the Anglo-American reception of French post-structuralism, in particular its understanding of the problem of identity. Readers will have to take the measure of this challenge on their own, but I will try to sketch its basis here in terms of how Nancy's reading of Kant opens out onto the problem of translation.

However, beyond the lag between its French publication and

its translation into English, there is also a properly *critical* reason why the specific difficulties of translating *Logodaedalus* do not merely stem from the empirical differences between vocabularies and grammars. Simply put, such disjunctions are never merely empirical. As the fact that this is a book about Kant might already suggest, there is a systematic—or at least a systemic, if not quite transcendental—reason that imposes itself on translation. *Logodaedalus* takes up the question of the latter's famously difficult prose as a problem that the presentation and exposition of critical philosophy posed first of all to Kant himself. As Nancy shows, the problem of how to write philosophy goes to the heart of the attempt to establish the autonomy of reason through the delineation of its limits; and this task is, in some manner—a *manner*, in fact, that is the very subject of this book—synonymous with saying in language what these limits are.

In other words, *Logodaedalus* is concerned with a certain problem of translation that inhabits critical philosophy at its core. Despite the fact that Kant takes mathematical demonstration as an ideal of presentation, he must translate the System into language, or *as* language. Walter Benjamin's conception of translation envisaged something quite similar when he argued in "The Task of the Translator" that translation was not so much a rendering of specific linguistic contexts, but of an intention toward language as a totality, or, to echo his famous essay, "language as such": "The task of the translator consists in finding the particular intention toward the target language which produces in that language the echo of the original. This is a feature of translation that basically differentiates it from the poet's work, because the intention of the latter is never directed toward the specific linguistic contextual aspects."[2] The System demands a prose of thought that is not an artful, beautiful prose, but that is an "architectonic," a pure structural presentation of itself as the blueprint of reason, what Benjamin calls *reine Sprache*, or "true language."[3] This demand, a demand for a style of presentation that is a style without style, produces what Nancy calls here the "syncope." The syncope imposes the distinction between philosophical presentation, *Darstellung*, and

Dichtung, what one might translate as Poesy, or even "invention," what Philippe Lacoue-Labarthe has rendered in French as "œuvre d'art." The syncope of discourse, of a philosophy obliged to write itself, produces the split between "philosophy" and "literature" that defines, in Nancy's view, modern thought in Kant's wake. But if the notion of "literature" and everything it implies in the way of style, form, and surface is a by-product of the program of critical philosophy, then translation, insofar as it concerns the transfer of the "content" of one language into the "form" of another language, is for this reason a *formal* practice of language, of form *as* matter, or content. Translation is thus implicated in Kant's attempt to articulate and present the limits of thought insofar as these limits define the totality of the system.

For our purposes here, what is important to say about this is that the Kantian demand for a philosophical style—a properly infinite task, as Nancy shows—also shapes the style and manner of Nancy's *Logodaedalus*, which is by no means merely an attempt to render Kant's "bad" writing into a more lucid prose, and thus into a "good" writing that would clarify and resolve, and thus somehow decide, for once and for all, the sense of the latter's thought. Rather, Nancy sets out to repeat and thus translate the Kantian syncope "itself." Consequently, a rigorous translation of *Logodaedalus* does not fulfill its task if it rests content with reproducing and expressing the meaning of the original text and even something of its style (though this is not to say that it does not attempt to do this, too). One must recognize and understand how Nancy translates the impossible presentation—that is, Kant's *prose*—and, therefore, how he reproduces the syncope. Such a syncope, as Nancy shows, does not simply lend itself to be read and thus translated; rather, it constitutes, as any reader of Kant might tell you, and as the many citations Nancy collects in this text amply testify, an experience of reading, and thus of writing and translating, that must itself be somehow transferred and repeated. Beyond the pragmatic concerns that make up the stuff of brackets and footnotes, it is this dimension of Nancy's text, his discursive practice, that requires some accounting for here, for it is also not without its logic.

A good way to begin to gain a sense of this discursive dimension of *Logodaedalus* is to consider an obvious example Nancy offers in the first pages of the Preamble, as if to alert the reader to what lies ahead on his road: the word *mode*, which takes both genders in French. There is *la mode*, fashion, and *le mode*, which can mean form, manner, mode, and method, the *way* of doing something (*methodos*), and which points to the philosophical notion of modality. Nancy's play on the difference in gender and sense between *le* and *la* mode points to a duality that characterizes both Kant's and his own text, to the superficial, accidental, and transitory dimension of fashion in its ever-changing superficiality *and* to the manner, method, or fashion of doing something that constitutes the very substance of philosophy as a scientific enterprise (its ideal, for Kant, let us not forget, is the method of proof in mathematics). Nancy thereby alerts his reader to an entire vocabulary of fashion that runs quietly yet persistently through this text—words like *allure, tenue, elegance* usually found on the pages of *Vogue* or *Mode* and not normally associated with the upright, stolid values and edifices of philosophical discourse—and which somehow translate the stuff of these from stone into something like *clothing,*or —what is eminently Kantian—into veils. In writing and inscribing Kant's text into this double register, into both the discourse of method and into the idiom of "popular," ordinary language, Nancy, like Kant, suspends the difference between "superficial" form and "deep" content, or substance, between fashion and method.

The name Nancy gives to this suspension is the "syncope," which I have chosen to translate with its English cognate, which has the three main senses of the French, though far less colloquially. In French, *avoir une syncope* means first of all "to pass out," "faint," "lose consciousness," or "black out"; it may even mean to experience a momentary stoppage of the heart or to miss a heartbeat. Second, a *syncope* is a rhetorical term indicating the suppression of a letter in the middle of a word. Third, it is a musical term indicating an interruption of the flow of a musical line, that is, a syncopation, a form identified generally with jazz (which Adorno found, let us recall, to be the avatar of a false aesthetic realization of subjective freedom, and thus the most insidious form of the instrumental power of the System). More colloquially, however, *avoir une syncope* also means in French "to have a heart attack," as when someone says, "I almost had a heart attack when I heard (. . .)!" This more popular and figurative usage points to the double register that constitutes the space of Nancy's discourse here, which demonstrates that the logical, grammatical, and thus normative level of language cannot be dissociated from the level of idiomatic language and the dimension of *tone* (*Stimmung*). In this manner, the syncope points to the corporeality (a heart attack!) of consciousness in its linguistic expression, the dimension and moment (transcendental? empirical? empirico-transcendental?) wherein consciousness senses or feels itself "in the flesh" and does so precisely because it is there that it blacks out, perhaps in the face of a sudden shock, a powerful emotion, or an experience of sublime grandeur—or just from trying to read Kant. It names the waking unconsciousness we call "incomprehension" that forces one to read a text over and over, especially when it operates, as does Nancy's, in multiple registers. It names, in other words, the impossibility of achieving a mathematical Darstellung that takes the form of an equation stating an identity. Translation becomes, therefore, the necessary attempt to produce a philosophical discourse in the wake of the impossibility of such a mathematical presentation.

However, Nancy also uses another term for this monstrous dimension of language that reminds us that the syncope is, in its violence, always related to an aesthetic moment: the *bon mot*, the joke, or the *Witz*, which for Kant is the prerogative of wit and genius. Nancy explores this notion at length both in this work and elsewhere.[4] In some respects, the bon mot organizes the text of *Logodaedalus* insofar as it names the language of the genius whose inventive power is necessary for the presentation of the System, but whom Kant also pushes aside as being too dangerous and too *aesthetic* for the style of critical philosophy. By embracing Witz, Nancy overturns Kant's fear of it by demoting it from being a prerogative of genius and putting it to work to do the manual labor of philosophical composition. The bon mot, in a sense, is a form of the syncope. There are several important words that recur throughout *Logodaedalus* and display and perform the work of the Witz. These include *décider*, *partager*, and *advenir*. Each of these, for its own specific reasons, went on to have a distinguished career in Nancy's later works. I have indicated where they arise, but I will restrict my comments about them to notes. However, the terms *exposé* and *exposition*, which are closely bound to Kant's German Darstellung, both deserve mention. Although Darstellung has been recently translated as "exhibition," I have chosen to remain with the more traditional translation, "presentation," and to translate exposé as "to present." In France, students make an exposé in class, that is, they make a presentation. I wanted to keep something of this everyday pedagogical meaning, for it is a motif that Nancy explicitly remarks in Kant's own comments about his writing (in his correspondence, moreover, with his translators). In addition, the notions of "ex-position" and of "being ex-posed" increasingly take center stage in Nancy's later writing, and I felt it would be important to offer readers a chance to see how they develop and emerge out of his reading of Kant and the problem of writing critical philosophy. For the French *exposition*, I have used its perfectly serviceable English cognate, though it is generally translated in English as an "exhibition." It implies a sensible manifestation and exposure. But I found it necessary to diverge from these in several instances in the name of lucidity and accuracy, and I have indicated where this is the case.

Perhaps the most important and emblematic display of Witz lies in Nancy's handling of the French idiom *tenir un discours*, which means "to speak" or to "make a speech." So much so, in fact, that one ought to hear the title *Discours de la syncope* first in the everyday sense of this expression: the *Speech of the Syncope*, or even the *Talk of the Syncope*, and only afterward in the more formal and perhaps academic sense of the English word *discourse*. Yet, tenir un discours may also mean that one "has," or "holds," a position, point of view, or idea, philosophical or ideological, in the sense that one masters and controls it, and thus upholds it, as one might in an academic, philosophical, or political context, or in the sense of control conveyed by the word *dictate*. Nancy plays frequently on and across the tension between these senses, and there is no English equivalent able to consistently convey all of them. I have chosen to translate the title literally as the *The Discourse of the Syncope*, largely because the complexity of the French here is actually available in the English, though it remains submerged, especially in academic usage. Furthermore, the verb *tenir* is itself one of the most complex in the French language, and its use with different prepositions makes up one of the longest entries in the dictionary, as well as one of the most difficult to "hear" for a nonnative ear. As a result, I have not adopted a standard English equivalent for the many ways Nancy turns it; however, I have indicated its presence in brackets where appropriate and provided notes to give the reader a sense of the different nuances and polarities of meaning it conveys in each instance.

The tension between high and low language I have here tried to describe—and which organizes to a great extent the *discursive logic* of *Logodaedalus*—corresponds quite closely, in fact, to the distinction Heidegger makes in *Being and Time* between "idle talk" (*Gerede*), the *chatter* and preunderstood language of *das Man*, and the resolute speech (*Rede*) of Dasein in its autoappropriation. The verb *tenir* and the expression "tenir un discours" further allude to the entire register of the "hand" that Heidegger deploys in *Being and Time*, and thus to the difference he posits in the practical attitude for which things are "ready-to-hand" (*Zuhandenheit*) and the theoretical attitude one adopts when something is merely "present-to-hand" (*Vorhandenheit*). Nancy is dialoguing not only with the "early" Heidegger but also with the late Heidegger of *On the Way to Language* (*Unterwegs zur Sprache*) where his conception of *Saying* privileges the *way* of saying over what is being "said" and thus points to the idea of a poetic discourse that cannot be reduced to predication and the positing of concepts. By inscribing the latter's famous "ways that lead nowhere" (in French: *chemins qui mènent nulle part*) back into Kant's modes (le and la mode), by activating the colloquial, ordinary dimensions of French, and by highlighting if not adopting a vocabulary of fashion—that quint-essentially French artifact of the modern urban metropole—Nancy is questioning and submitting Heidegger's claim that language is "the house of being" to the exigency of translation. Yet he is doing it on the basis of the latter's own conception of the *way*. In this gesture, Nancy pushes Kant toward Heidegger and Heidegger toward Kant. The implication is that the discourse of the syncope occurs precisely between the "form" of *critique* and the "content" of fundamental ontology.

I would like to close with a brief discussion of one last issue of translation. In the Preamble, Nancy makes use of a prepositional phrasing with no real English equivalent: " . . . à même le texte de Kant." As Céline Surprenant, the translator of *The Speculative Remark: (One of Hegel's Bon Mots)*, has noted, *à même* is related to Hegel's "in itself" (*an sich*), which she chose to translate as "just at the level."[5] I have chosen a perhaps less elegant, and simpler formulation: "*on and in Kant's text itself*" [à même le texte de Kant], in order to highlight the effective dimension of this inscription. With this term, it seems, Nancy indicates that the syncope should not be misunderstood as positing any kind of dialectical relation; rather, à même points to a relation of sameness that does not imply an absence of difference. The syncope and its discourse articulate a difference of the *same* between a critical analytic philosophy and a fundamental ontology. If Nancy leads Heidegger back to Kant's critical *methodos*, and if he does so by the former's own insistence on Saying and on the *Way*, and yet against him in a most singular repetition of the critical gesture, the subtlety of this "method" can only be admired. The textual syncopation of the *same* on its way, the way upon which it attempts to constitute itself out of itself, is a practice of repetition and translation that recasts and translates both Heidegger's late poetizing and Kant's critical philosophy one through the other. In other words, critique translates critique and thus demands and implies an understanding and a practice of translation. It is for this reason that to read Nancy, one must always read him with a dual insight, stereoscopically, to borrow a Benjaminian notion, for that is how he conceives of Critique: it doubles and reproduces itself, or writes in *stereo*, as it were, reproducing itself as "literature" and turning Kant, as Nancy shows, into a character who haunts modern literature. To read Nancy, we must not only understand him, we must also listen to him as well. The reader will have to weigh to what extent an English translation of *Logodaedalus* succeeds or fails to make this possible.

Finally, a word needs to be said regarding the translations of the citations that punctuate and syncopate the text of *Logodaedalus*. Whenever available, I have tried to supply the most current existing English translation, especially of Kant's texts. Every effort has been made to provide references for even the briefest of citations; however, in a few cases, I have been unable to track down sources. I have also modified a number of existing translations in order to better convey something legible in the French and thus important to the intelligibility of Nancy's commentary, but not conveyed by the existing translation.

I have sought to produce a translation that is both "literal" and faithful to the "spirit" of this text. In this respect, I have tried whenever possible to maintain the integrity of Nancy's sentences in the interest of conveying something of the rhythm of his prose, which is highly marked and constitutes a discursive element that the English-speaking reader should be aware of. Nancy's sentences pause, digress, comment, and return upon themselves. Or they merely begin in medias res, as if out of nothing and nowhere. The *logodaedalus*, according to Kant, is a "grammarian" "who quibbles over words," but as Nancy shows us, he does not quibble only over their sense but also over their order, their periods, and their rhythm.

Saul Anton
Paris, January 2007

Preface

Saul Anton, who has taken upon himself the task of translating this book—a task rendered more thankless by the necessity of tracking down the English translations of all the citations inserted in the text—has asked me how *Logodaedalus* appears to me, now, thirty years later, a work belonging in some way to my "youth" and also to the youth of a thinking preoccupied by what one could then call the relation between literature and philosophy, or, to say it more rigorously, the question of the philosophical text—or, to be more rigorous still, and thus to speak German, the question of philosophical Darstellung. How does thinking exhibit itself, present itself? How does the science of principles and ends take on form and embody itself in the order of language?

If this question preoccupied us then, it is because it articulated in a manner that was still relatively restrained and actually timid the more serious question of knowing just how far and how the thought of principles and ends, or rather, the thought of Being and beings as such—in short, metaphysics—can be totally consistent without also thinking—and radically—the implication of its object (let us say "being" to be brief) in its action, in this act of thinking that is nothing other than speaking. However, the act of speaking is in turn nothing but the act of writing, if *writing*—a term thus promoted to the status of a regulative idea—designates nothing but cutting a path to the nongivenness of "sense," to this not-yet-signified and to this not-yet-said which alone, in truth, opens language, which alone opens it *to truth*, and which knows itself from the outset to forever be unable to arrive at something like a goal, a conclusion, a Sense.

Knowing itself to be so, this act also knows itself as the very inscription of truth, truth insofar as it is its inscription: the truth that is true only as its own tracing [*tracé*], and thus not merely as its own way, as it is for Plato, Descartes, and Hegel, but more than the way, the *trace* [trace], foreign to ideas of route and destination, and fated essentially to efface itself without essence. The way, in effect, the track of methodos, but thought as a lost way, overgrown with grass and brambles, soon to be indiscernible from the thicket. More adventurous, in short, than even Heidegger's "ways that lead nowhere" [*Holzwege*].

This question, or this program of questioning and concern, has lost nothing of its appeal and its exigency for me. On the contrary, everything has intensified: philosophy has not ceased, in all its living and nonregressive forms, in all its courageous, impatient forms, to sharpen the point. Nothing less than the following: we are learning to take care, certainly still of "being" or of "principles" and "ends," but in order to do so, first of voices, languages, modes of address, and even of song (or of exclamation, of prayer, of fervor, or anger) *by which, in which*, or better still, *as which*, can arrive things such as some "being," "principles," "truth," or "reason" in general.

In a word: from one end to the other, philosophy knows itself to be called out on [*interpelée*] its *poetic* capacity, that is to say, on its ability *to create*—concepts or words, tones or even voices, modulations or timbres. In other words, this ability is addressed just as much in its musicality [*interpellée*], and the question could be formulated as follows: How do we *interpret* that which philosophy imparts [*partage*]?

We know that this questioning [*interpellation*], the seed of which is already there in Plato, but which knew after him a very long incubation, has been reactivated in a hundred ways after Kant.

It is, in certain respects, the proper mark of thought in modern history.

That is why, today, I understand even better how it is that I was so intrigued by and attracted to the very singular relation that Kant entertained with his own writing, his deprecation of his prosaic character and the hope that he nourished of seeing develop in others a poetic metamorphosis. To which was added for me the following singular motif, which sets apart the figure of Kant as a literary object: no other philosopher has found a place in so many texts of fiction or poetry.

After the publication of the book in 1976, I received from certain readers other examples of this singular destiny. I'll cite the following quote by Artaud:

> Mr. Kant was a little girl who wanted to be a poet in his way and whose jealousy of beings forced him to limit himself exclusively to philosophy.[1]

One can also find attestations to the opposite, like that of Walter Benjamin, who wrote in a letter dated October 22, 1917: "Kant's prose per se represents a *limes* of literary prose."[2] But the inversion of meaning here is only apparent: because he perceives in Kant a yet-unheard-of philosophical stake, still to come, Benjamin wishes to receive his prose—usually judged to be heavy—as if possessing artistic force, that is to say, the force of awakening, indeed of enthusiasm. Moreover, he immediately adds, "If this were not the case, would the *Critique of Pure Reason* have so shaken Kleist to the deepest parts of his being?"

Yet that is precisely what we want, too: that philosophy shake us to the most profound parts of ourselves, not by poetic flatteries, but rather by the trembling that must always produce anew the eruption of the possibility of sense, the imminence of a truth in the process of flowing forth. What Kant experienced in his desire for poetry was the tension in a joy without which truth is merely conformity, a *jouissance*—fainting and rapture [*transport*]—without which reason does not make any room for the unconditioned.

The world is probably less inclined today to get excited about the thought of a philosophical enthusiasm than it was thirty years ago. But thirty years ago, this world did not yet know itself to be "globalized," and our exuberances remained largely those of the old children of Europe. They can today become those of mature young people who discover a new source for an ever-renewable admiration: no longer merely for the starry sky above nor only the moral law in our hearts, but a new world to be made in front of us.

Jean-Luc Nancy
Christmas, 2006

Considered from the proper point of view, all philosophy is nothing but human understanding placed in an amphigouric language.

—Goethe, posthumous maxim

For there are many to whom I yield precedence in knowledge of philosophy, but if I lay claim to the orator's peculiar ability to speak with propriety, clearness, elegance, I think my claim is in a measure justified, for I have spent my life in the profession. . . . I believe, of course, that if Plato had been willing to devote himself to forensic oratory, he could have spoken with the greatest eloquence and power, and that if Demosthenes had continued the studies he pursued with Plato and had wished to expound his views, he could have done so with elegance and brilliance. I feel the same way about Aristotle and Isocrates, each of whom, engrossed in his own profession, undervalued that of the other.

—Cicero, *On Duties* (*De officiis*)

The Philosopher spends his life in observing men and uses his mind to tease out the vices and ridicule. If he gives his thoughts any figurative turn, it's less by authorial necessity than in order to lend it a vanity that he daily found necessary in order to serve his design.

—Jean de La Bruyère, *Characters*

Philosophy is distinguished from other kinds of knowledge only by its form.

—Immanuel Kant, posthumous note

There is no book that one doesn't read with pleasure when it has a beautiful style. In Philosophy proper, however austere it may be, some manners are expected. This is not without its reasons; since, as I believe I've said elsewhere, eloquence is in the sciences what the sun is in the world. Knowledge is only shadows if those who deal in it do not know how to write.

—Père Lamy, *Rhetoric: Or the Art of Speaking*

Let us not make fun either of the one who does philosophy as a philosopher, since the former is only a workman (it would be to mistake the versifier for the original genius).

—Immanuel Kant, *Opus postumum*

I placed highest the art of the philosopher in the philosopher who renounces being one, who doesn't dress his windows, neither as a writer nor as a man, in order to reveal the philosopher he is, who is happy to be one according to its essence not its form.

—Ludwig Feuerbach, *The Essence of Christianity*

It is entirely evident that certain barbaric, un-German, and circuitous language ornaments philosophy more than it disfigures it: Oracles despise charm, Vox dei soloecismus: in other words, a Kantian is not to be read but rather only studied.

—Jean Paul, *The Valley of Kampan*

Kantian philosophy reveals its nature and its purpose in its very neglected narrative.

—G. W. F. Hegel, *Faith and Knowledge*

Because who was more of a philosopher than Kant?

—Alexander Kojève, *Kant*

Carried along by his throng of thoughts, delivered over to the ease of combining them, and forced to produce, [the philosophical genius] finds a thousand specious proofs and is unable to assure himself of any of them. He builds sturdy buildings that reason would not dare to live in and that please him by their proportions rather than by their solidity. He admires his systems like he admires the layout of a poem, and he adopts them as beautiful, in believing he loves them as if they were true. The true and the false are hardly the distinctive characteristics of the genius.

—Denis Diderot, "Art," *Encyclopedia*

THE DISCOURSE OF THE SYNCOPE

§ 1   Preamble: The Discourse of the Syncope

It is not enough to say that there is undecidability in a discourse. It is not enough to say it in order to have decided the outcome, the structure, or the potency of the discourse in question. Today, just about everywhere, one finds "undecidability" as a solution, one that some would gladly substitute for the well-worn answers of such-and-such "truth," or for Truth as such. My concern in this book will thus be to not allow the crisis that has been inaugurated by what is called "undecidability" somewhere in discourse, in every *discourse*, to be redirected or collapsed back into a *solution*.

But perhaps this is to go too quickly to the "theme" of my essay, of which this book is only the first part.[1] It's possible that it is better to take a more indirect approach, one that starts by circumscribing the program of the work to be done here. To do so, it is necessary to invoke or point to a kind of *disequilibrium*.

A Digression on Fashion

This necessity does not stem from today's widespread and perhaps trite predilection for the motives and values of rupture, collapse, and lack in all their forms, which are opposed to continuity, plenitude, solidity, and so on. Nowadays, a certain theoretical apparatus organizes its discourse, whatever it might be, in the name of the prefixes *de-*, *in-*, *dis-*, or *dys-*, not to mention the *trans-* and

the *para-*, as if governed by an unassailable obligation. The most
trivial, the most self-satisfied, and shortsighted criticism does not
shy away from pointing out these features in order to ridicule
them. There is no question here of collaborating with and affirming this kind of criticism (nor even of talking about them, for they
do not merit discussion). Although that which can give rise to
a fashion [*la mode*] is never without its necessity, this one is not
necessarily the substantial and univocal necessity of an Absolute or
a History. And yet, to have contempt for fashion, it is necessary
to have inherited some self-confidence, even some powerful and
intransigent metaphysics: namely, one must be a Hegelian of strict
observance. A text by Hegel will prove this, and not by chance is
this text directed against the Cynics, the guerrillas of philosophy
that the System and its Science cannot properly put up with:

> Socrates hence declares the clothing of the
> Cynics to be vanity. . . . Clothing is not a
> thing of rational import, but is regulated
> through needs that arise of themselves. The
> clothing in the North must be different from
> the clothing worn in Central Africa, and in
> winter we do not wear cotton garments. Any-
> thing beyond this is meaningless and is left
> to chance and opinion; in modern times, for
> instance, old-fashioned clothing had a mean-
> ing in relation to patriotism. The cut of my
> coat is decided by fashion, and the tailor sees
> to this; it is not my business to invent it, for
> mercifully, others have done so for me. This
> dependence on custom and opinion is cer-
> tainly better than were it to be a dependence
> on nature. But it is not essential that men
> should direct their understanding to this; in-
> difference is the point of view that must reign
> in regards to clothing, since the thing itself is
> undoubtedly perfectly indifferent.[2]

What can set off a trend [*des effets de mode*] is thus not without its necessity, but this necessity does not belong to fashion [*la mode*] as such. By contrast, fashion *as such*, or, to be more precise, thinking of something as *fashion* [la mode], should not be separated from the thought of mode [*du mode*], to which it is tied by a bond that is as much metaphysical as it is etymological and semantic. In other words, the thought of substance. Fashion [*la mode*] and mode [*le mode*] are twin figures of the idea of variation on the basis of an underlying truth, nature, or substance. There is probably no *mode* [*pas de* mode] properly speaking—with everything that this word connotes about aesthetics, society, and economics—except in a society structured by Western metaphysics. And fashion trends consist precisely in that they hark back to the system of substance. In short, let us say that today the trend consists in an entirely new kind of transubstantiation of everything that—by means of another necessity—consumes and undoes the system of substance. The signs pointing to the decomposition, deconstruction, displacement, or the overflow of this system—in other words, of the whole architectonic and history of the West—that are called, for example (but in whittling down the meaning of these nouns) "text," "signifier," "lack," "drift," "trace," and so on are converted into values and thereby erected into truths and hypostasized into substances.—In a certain way, this transubstantiation is inevitable (and also what makes this digression necessary . . .): this conversion is prescribed by the economy itself of the very first discourses to advance these signs and not merely in what has been repeated or pillaged by epigones. It is due to [*tient à*] the *economy* of discourse, which can neither function without the *value* (of truth), nor without fetishizing general equivalence as the basis on which values can be distinguished and exchanged. And discourse insists on this, and will insist upon it for a long time to come, as far as the eye can see (as long as the system of *sight*, of *theory*). At least one dimension of what goes by the name of "theory" today must lie, with an ever-rekindled urgency, in undoing the economy that reconstitutes itself, in doing so as much in the discourse of fashion as much as in that of its adversary—(and thus also in the discourse of the syncope).

A task for Penelope, one might say, though perhaps not destined to reconstitute a domestic economy. We know that Odysseus's homecoming—the return of the *same* Odysseus to the *same* place, his final *home*—is precisely what for a long time has placed into question the whole of our fantasmatic of return, of voyage, and of drift.

Three Disequilibriums

It is a question here, therefore, of work that is unbalanced, or, to be more precise, that is itself worked—eaten-away, undermined— by a triple disequilibrium:

>—*Of the object*: This can be designated as the Kantian theory of schematism; however, if this "theory" is indeed an essential piece, indeed the cornerstone of Kantian theory in general (on this point, the Heideggerian "repetition" of Kant as well as Roger Daval's attempt to reorganize the whole of Kantianism around the notion of the schema are indisputable), a first disequilibrium immediately takes shape: it is impossible to separate out from it an object called a "schema"; it brings along with it the whole of Kant's discourse. We cannot disguise this necessity, which does not imply—far from it—that we are obligated to here undertake a global interpretation of Kantianism. Rather, it implies something less ambitious but more restrictive: namely, that we must manage to touch at the *very* structure, foundation, and locus of a discourse. In turn, this demand only comes fully into view because of a second disequilibrium. As we know already, the "theory" of the schema also happens to constitute the blind spot of Kantian theory. The moment one ceases to engage oneself in its interpretation, there is no longer any chance of shedding light on it. In all these ways, the treatment of the object, here, remains at a slight remove or superimposed upon this object.

>—*Of discourse*: This follows from what we have just said. The existence of a blind spot that is constitutive of all theory—just as it is constitutive of the eye and of vision—is well established. As a result, the desire to produce a theory of schematism is like setting up, if not a dialogue of the deaf, then a face-to-face encounter of the blind. And yet, my discourse here, as discourse, cannot pretend to be anything

other than theoretical.—In fact this is precisely why the theoretical must itself be in play here. It is by looking at itself that it unbalances itself. The true stake is in no longer entirely *holding* a discourse, neither as one holds a tool, nor as one holds to—that is, keeps—one's word. Such is the real—and, so to speak, *concrete*—enterprise of this work in all its generality. This doesn't mean that Kant is purely a pretext here. What is at stake and what has been in play since 1789,[3] is precisely the exhibition of theory's face-to-face encounter with itself, and the exhausting, unbalancing question of the refinement [*la tenue*] of its discourse.

—*Of economy.* The question of schematism will not arise right away. On the contrary, in this first volume, it will begin to crop out only toward the end.[4] An entire first pass—deprived in some sense of its "final" theoretical justifications—is needed to consider the position, program, and *genre* of Kantian discourse. *Logodaedalus* confronts schematism only from the perspective of the problem that the elegance of his style posed to Kant. We shall discover, moreover, that this problem would never arise for a thought that does not require a theory of schematism. However, we shall also discover that this theory would have had no place in a discourse that was untroubled by the question of its presentation. There is thus a circular economy here, as there should be; however, it is not really able to achieve closure. Somehow, the question of "literature" remains extrinsic to, scattered, and without any real effect on the question of schematism—no more so than does Kant's will to systematicity succeed in imposing itself over his own writing. A certain shattering of purposes, a certain inability of taking command of one by the other compels the division between *Logodaedalus* and *Kosmotheoros*, as a syncope within this work itself.

The Enigma of the Same

Of the syncope, it is thus time, now, to speak—insofar as the main title of the work points to a single and general thing. Something that is not obvious.

Let us start over from the following: it is not enough to say that "there is undecidability" in a discourse, for example, in the discourse of Kant. It is even less sufficient in that it is precisely his discourse—and we shall see that it is his "interest"—that itself

marks this undecidability. To the two questions that summarize
the two stages of this work (questions posed by Kant and not to
Kant)—how to present philosophy and what holds up [*qu'est-ce
qui fait tenir*] the system?—we shall answer, taking a hasty short-
cut, that Kant "responds" with "undecidability." We shall further
add that these answers are not injected into Kant's discourse by
our interpretation, but rather are themselves marked by it. (Again,
it is necessary here to dispel any equivocation: we are not claiming
to do without interpretation, but these are henceforth inscribed
right on and in Kant's text itself [*inscrites à même le texte de Kant*]
and, above all, in Heidegger's, to which we shall get to. At the
same time, the history of interpretations of Kant is different from
that of all others. If one excludes doctrinaire "neo-Kantian" para-
phrasings, to speak quickly, it is a history of a series of questions
opened, reopened, gaping, or hanging, confronted with which one
stumbles, evades, sublimates, or loses oneself. It is the repetition
of this Kantian aporia that it is a question of . . . repeating.) In
every place that it systematically ties itself together, Kant's discourse marks its undecidability. We cannot rest content, therefore,
in "discovering" this undecidability. The problems to set out are
rather the following: What comes of a discourse that marks its
own undecidability?—And perhaps above all: Is the mark of undecidability a general discursive function? Indeed, in the final instance (yet how do we fix this "final" instance?), isn't the function
of discourse to execute this mark by means of an operation that is
neither merely a rupture *nor* merely a suture?

As we can see, these problems are nothing new today. Indeed.
It is only a question of repeating them with a certain insistence in
order to bring them to bear on *discourse*. The "transubstantiation"
of fashion consists too often in making discourse's undecidability appear before itself, in presenting it (and, hence, in making
one believe that one has mastered it) as an instance—a force, a
figure, a thing, what have you—that comes to it from outside.
(For example, when one attributes it to a "writing" conceived as
being simply and radically heterogeneous to discourse, a gesture
that arises from a "transubstantiation" of the concept—that is not

a concept—of "archi-writing" that Derrida has succeeded in producing and developing. An analogous operation can be performed on "laughter" in Bataille, or on "jouissance" in Lacan, and so on.) However, by doing so, and against the very intentions that one believes one is remaining faithful to, one preserves—or, worse still, reconstitutes or reinforces—this *outside* by means of which discourse has always assured its self-preservation through designating and fixing it. Let us say, with Nietzsche, that one is thereby working, without always having wanted it (?) [*sic*], to broaden and extend the shadow of God, and of metaphysics. Yet Nietzsche, so far as he was concerned, conspired to operate more implacably, more inexorably, at the heart *itself* of metaphysics. In the *Gay Science*, the construction of the Cartesian subject, the death of God, and the adventurous travels of the "free spirit" are all played out in the *same* place, on the *same* infinite ocean. This enigma of the *same* still remains—if not to be thought, then in every instance to be unremittingly expended in the discourse that bears it and which it sustains. Without which, rebalanced and reinforced, rearmed one by the other, discourse and its other perpetuate their mutual institution—that is, their philosophical, social, moral, political, and economic institution. (With what else do we have to *do* here?)

This task, less production than expenditure, or simultaneously expenditure and production, requires that one take a few precautions with the undecidable. One must carefully distinguish it, for example, from the saturating and reassuring function of the *ineffable*, which every discourse carries. One must also distinguish it from the position [*position*] of an equivocation or a fundamental ambiguity that would open in discourse a profusion and multiplicity of meanings that thrive from their intrinsic set of interconnections. These are all roles played by metaphysical truth—and all convert a lack or an absence, circumscribed by discourse, into the plenitude of a true outside, hanging out beyond discourse but surreptitiously controlled by it and by the discursive conditions of the production of the outside itself. On the contrary, one cannot sufficiently ponder (and even so, isn't this the *same* thing?), one cannot ruminate enough, or wear out the following remark by Bataille: "Only language reveals, at the limit, the sovereign moment when it no longer has any currency. But in the end the one who speaks owns up to his impotence."[5] In effect, it's *almost* the same thing; however, does the *same* take place by way of the *almost*? Therein lies the whole question. . . . In speaking these sentences, Bataille is making a speech [*tient un discours*]. What else would he do? In speaking these sentences, discourse must deny them; yet in so denying them, it would have to repudiate itself; it is obligated to hold them [*tenir*], and they are untenable [*intenable*].[6]

It's neither in vain nor by chance that we shall recall the origin of the word "undecidable." It comes from meta-mathematics, from a question that arises at the heart of the *model* of *mathesis*, out of Platonic-Cartesian knowledge (even if its coordinates are no longer "Cartesian"). If one imports this concept into philosophy (that is, perhaps, if one reimports the very mark of the co-belonging of mathematics and metaphysics), one ought not water down the structure so that it becomes a baggy and diffuse ambiguity. The undecidable is not louche, however one understands the term: what is dubious, what is of ill repute, and what is not without a certain charm. By contrast, the undecidable is made from the exact superimposition—in geometry they say homography—of the blind spot and the center of vision. An undecidable proposition is one that cannot be the object of any demonstration, neither by deducing it nor by excluding it from the system [*pour l'en exclure*]; it can neither be derived nor refuted; it does not submit to the logic of a system, though neither does it oppose it (since it belongs to it). We know that Gödel demonstrated that it is always possible to construct an undecidable proposition in a formal system—and thus the general impossibility of deciding a system, of establishing noncontradiction and completion on the basis of itself alone. But what counts here is not the failure of mathematical autodemonstration and the metaphysical nostalgia that it evokes. Rather, what counts, so to speak, is the autodemonstration of the failure.[7] The undecidable proposition is produced, marked, and classified by the system and within it.

Synthesis Syncope (-ates)

The enigma of the *same* is likely bound to the position and the affirmation of the undecidable: it's the *same* that produces and inscribes the undecidable, and that consequently controls it as one of its propositions or functions, and it is from the *same* that the inscription of the undecidable denies the possibility of assuring its identity without a remainder. The undecidable is the very power of the same—that which, by means of discourse, withdraws discourse from its own Absolute Knowledge. In this manner, the undecidable's emergence (as such) in the field of "meta-mathematics"—or, if you will, the problem of the "foundation of mathematics"—is likely precisely what started the definitive withdrawal of mathematics from questions about the *meta*physics of Self-Knowledge [*Savoir-de-soi*] and foundation. But it is discursivity as a whole that this operation is concerned with. The relation between discourse and mathematics dating "from time immemorial" repeats itself, and, in repeating itself, this *same* relation is displaced. Here, mathematics does not alight into its autonomy, abandoning the vain oversight of a bloodless philosophy (this is a scene that is still performed only in certain academic discourses . . .); rather, it brings along with it the general program that always jointly determined mathesis and metaphysics, knowledge and science.[8] (We shall see shortly how these rules begin to twist under the pressure of the Kantian question of presentation.) Because the undecidable is not the Other of the Same, the Other coming to poke holes into the Same in order to turn it into a specular *abyme* or an epiphany.

That which founds, that which supports, must it not "itself" be *insupportable*? This necessity belongs to all metaphysical ontologic, and, at the *same* [même] time, it is also its radical deterioration—or rather, it is the deterioration of the root *itself* [même]. Here, at least, one can forego negative or distorting prefixes: the *same itself* does insidious violence to the discourse of the same; it eats away at it and devastates it. The undecidable is the sameness of the same produced by the same as its alteration. This alteration does not possess the fertile negativity of the dialectical Other in the Same: it is the impossibility "itself" of the same. Or, if you want, it is the dialectic of the Same, and therefore the dialectic itself, as its own impossibility.[9] In the end, it's better to not say that the undecidable is this or that, and even that it is insupportable. Perhaps the least untenable statement is something along the lines of: *the same undecides itself.* The same undecides itself: it undoes itself as it constitutes itself, fissures itself in the very gesture and instant in which it overcomes, fixes, and effaces its fissures. *At the same time*: we shall see later that therein lies the whole structure of Kantian schematism. We shall avoid writing: "it fissures (itself)," or "there is no Self to which this action can be attributed." This is because it is precisely in this claim that the self of the same—its aseity—lies.

Thus, what is called consciousness probably never allows itself to be grasped as an identity except when it blacks out: it is the syncope. The syncope decides self-identity. It marks it as irrefutable in the gesture by which and the instant in which it is subtracted from all demonstration—and, above all, from all autodemonstrations, autopresentations or presencings. It should be understood that when we say "the syncope determines," it is by antiphrasis. The syncope is not anything and has no power. It is not a negative movement from one moment to the next, nor is it a whole that serves as a bridge. The syncope has, to be very exact, the instantaneous, punctual, and discrete (in the mathematical sense) nature of the *cogito*, and it is understood, furthermore, that if it's not the cogito, neither is there a cogito without one. The syncope *simultaneously* attaches and detaches (in Greek, for example, the suppression of a letter in a word; in music, a strong beat over silence). Of course, these two operations do not add up to anything, but neither do they cancel each other out. There remains the syncope itself, the same syncopated, that is to say, cut to pieces (its first meaning) *and* somehow rejoined through amputation. *The same is erected here through its resection*: the undecidable figure called "castration" derives from this.

This does not mean that we have just delivered ourselves over to an existential phenomenology of the syncope. If ever such a thing counted as a psychological consciousness, or even a meta-psychological one, it could only ever do so if it already derived from something equivalent to a transcendental "consciousness." Or, rather, to the transcendental *same.* The syncope is the equivalent of transcendental synthesis, which is why Kantian theory, the theory of synthesis as such, the theory of the production of identity, is here unavoidable. The syncope is not the reverse or the opposite of synthesis. Just as one has to say that the same undecides itself, one has to say that synthesis syncopates itself, its own thesis, and its own discourse. Or, that it's the syncope that "speaks" [*tient le discours*] the discourse of synthesis, which is thus simultaneously spoken [*tenu*] and not upheld [*non tenu*].[10] Or even, and very simply, if one dares say it in this way, one should say that *synthesis syncopates.*

Kantian philosophy stems from [*tient à*] this undecidability and keeps to this syncope. It announces and notes it, and in doing so, it identifies itself in what is most proper to it *and* dooms its transcendental identity, its *own* system, to impossibility. Here is what it ought be a question of in the pages that follow. To say it in another way, fundamentally, it should be a question of the systematic, permanent, and "synthetic" collapse of the very foundation of discourse.

And consequently, it must be a question of the mode of inscription or the mode of production of the undecidable. But only in such a way that it is accepted from the beginning that there is no "I" that prepares or plans the syncope, nor any organization or productive finality that gives itself the undecidable. And yet, it is the same that syncopates, the same that undecides itself. One could say: *id* syncopates.[11] But only on the condition that one does not think of the id as the vague and indistinct force of a primordial origin, an ultimate instance that comes to determine everything. The id could be chaos—one runs across chaos more than once in Kant. But once more, on the condition of insisting on the following—which doesn't let itself be thought and which exhausts thought: chaos is not chaotic (supposing that "the chaotic" can even be made to function as a quality or a predicate) if, erected as the primordial Other, it resolves and dissolves the question of the same. Chaos is chaotic insofar as it *is* the same (the same as the same). It's not only in mythology that chaos has its own name and possesses the active power of generation all the while being external to all regimes of order and all generative processes. *Chaos* is perhaps the proper name itself, the name of the Same that inscribes its syncope—and, as a result, the "mythological" name that "logic" failed to diminish. The syncope happens to the proper, the proper, the same, comes about [*advient*]—undecides itself—in syncopation.

Something Repulsive to Look At

The question of the production of undecidability, which is also the question of an undecidable production, that is, the question of the "agent" of philosophical inscription as a syncopated agent—or, more precisely, the question of philosophy as the question of the *philosopher*, of the philosopher who has passed out (if one tries to hear "the philosopher" neither as a subjective entity nor as an empirical individual); or, to ask this in another way: Who or what philosophizes? Who decides or undecides?—This question, which displaces, transforms, and reinitiates *all* the theoretical and practical questions that can be linked to philosophical discourse; or, rather, if one so desires, by way of a loaded word that's very hard to put into play (we shall return to this, too), this question of the *flesh* of philosophy, of the flesh and bone of philosophy, in effect, of philosophical incarnation—this question of the philosopher, therefore, it bears repeating, belongs to Kant.

Kant did not make it a "privileged object" of his work. Rather, one might say that it's all he did. In Kantian discourse, it is *the* discourse of metaphysics that undecides itself, and it's *the* philosopher who blacks out [*syncope*]. And we should not rush to say that this has always happened in the course of philosophy. Not that it isn't true. But it is just as true—it is truth *itself*—that the syncope happens, that there are philosophical events and histories that syn-

copate History. It happened to Kant. Hegel was not mistaken on
the matter:

> Identity of this formal kind finds itself im-
> mediately confronted by or next to an infi-
> nite nonidentity, with which it must coalesce
> in some incomprehensible way. On one side
> there is the Ego, with its productive imagina-
> tion or rather with its synthetic unity which,
> taken thus in isolation, is formal unity of the
> manifold. But next to it there is an infinity of
> sensations and, if you like, of things in them-
> selves. Once it is abandoned by the categories,
> this realm cannot be anything but a formless
> lump, even though, according to the *Critique
> of Judgment*, it is a realm of beauteous nature
> and contains determinations with respect to
> which judgment cannot be subsumptive but
> only reflecting. Objectivity and stability de-
> rive solely from the categories; the realm of
> things in themselves is without categories;
> yet it is something for itself and for reflec-
> tion. The only idea we can form of this realm
> is like that of the iron king in the fairy tale
> whom a human self-consciousness permeates
> with the veins of objectivity so that he can
> stand erect. But then formal transcendental
> idealism sucks these veins out of the king so
> that the upright shape collapses and becomes
> something in between form and lump, re-
> pulsive to look at. For the cognition of na-
> ture, without the veins injected into nature
> by self-consciousness, there remains nothing
> but sensation. —G. W. F. Hegel, *Faith and
> Knowledge*

What metaphysical discourse cannot stand, what disgusts it, is
the syncope. *Speculation* requires the live subject, ready and standing erect in its mirror; it also recognizes itself in the simple re-

versal of the mirror, in the smooth and absolute black of its tain. It refuses and rejects (which is to say, it also always *comprehends*, assumes and sublimates, sublates or attempts to sublate, one must not forget) the slackening, the loss of blood, the loss of sense, the between-life-and-death that is always too close. This episode is not only played out between Kant and Hegel; it is constantly re-played; the play of discourse consists in replaying it. That's why the "Kant" who appears in this book is not an object of the past—in the name of erudition, of the history of philosophy, or of who knows which priceless "return to Kant." Kant—*kant*, one has the urge to write—his proper name, almost a noun, just like the name of Chaos (and, as we shall see, having spread all the way to litera-ture), has not ceased to punctuate, since Kant, and to syncopate, the history of discourse.[12] It is in the name of this that he plays a part here—in the guise of the kant [*le kant*] that undecides itself in every discourse. Moreover—we have already said so and the second volume will return to this—it is impossible to take on kant without taking on its repetitions, above all Heidegger's. However, what needs to be examined in Heidegger and in his kant [*le kant*] is precisely the repetition of the undecidable, of the syncope. Nev-ertheless, it should not be forgotten—and we will have occasion to recall—that Heidegger's repetition of Kant is nothing but the rep-etition of the repetition of Kant in Nietzsche, in Husserl, and—no matter how surprising or, by contrast, academic it appears—prob-ably in Marx and in Freud.

Ultimately, all ventures on the kant [*le kant*] slip. They can but only undecide themselves in turn. It has been said that this implies two questions: It's "known"—though what kind of knowledge is this?—that neither one nor the other has an answer, that these questions themselves are programmed by the undecidable. Who would be naive enough to want to hold the discourse of undecid-ability? Insisting on it is exhausting and hopeless in principle, yet in a way that can hardly be said to be tragic (it is rather the mat-ter of a certain laughter). And yet, who would want to renounce it? Or rather: Who would have the naiveté to believe in the pure and simple disappearance of philosophy—and of the philosopher?

That is to say, of history? A great outburst of laughter can answer this question; laughter is still a syncope. What prescription, what imperative is in command here? Could there be a *duty* here? A duty to discourse that would no longer owe anything to the discourse (which undecides itself) of values and knowledge? In what unprecedented sense, in what sense irreducible to the mode of *de*- could there be a morality of *unhope* [dés-espoir]?

In Summary

Philosophical discourse is pronounced over a syncope or by a syncope. It is held up [*tenu*] by an undecidable moment of syncope. This moment, this mode of production, and this regime of inscription are Kant's, which means: they are Kant's *still today*. The Kantian function in philosophy is what exhibits—or should one say *incises?*—the syncope, in spite of everything, in spite of all the will in discourse. Philosophy has always comprised this function, even if it is constitutionally incapable of understanding it (and why, at the critical moment, the syncope happens to it). Philosophy has always known that it possessed what is untenable. That's why it denies it and pretends to know or to think. It even pretends to think what is untenable. And, therefore, that is why it exasperates itself and makes discourse tremble over this "Kantian function" (the one who doesn't tremble is not the philosopher, but rather the philosophical ideologue, whomever and whatever he or she may be or claim to be—conservative, reformist, or destroyer of philosophy). There is no point in doing philosophy if it isn't to try to accompany this exhaustion of discourse to its limit. Because it is only at the limit that one can try philosophy's luck: its stake is not that of an "interest" but rather of an injunction, a prescription, a strange *you must discourse* that has nourished it and is now wearing out the history of an entire civilization. Intervention into this history passes by way of this limit.

In Kant, this *"you must"* takes the form of the necessity, however unresolved, of schematism, which is the condition for the production of sense. This necessity gives rise to two questions: First, *how to present philosophy?* (This is the question of style, of literature in philosophy.) Second, *what "speaks" "holds up" the system* [qu'est-ce qui fait « tenir »]? (This is the question of the schema, of its figure and its ethos.) *Logodaedalus* asks the first as an angle of attack on the second, to which we will return in *Kosmotheoros*.

I am not claiming here to speak or to *deploy* the discourse of the syncope. Neither is anyone pretending to dance on the ruins of a philosophical Carthage. However, there is someone here asking themselves what is offered by and what *must* still be articulated by the dead philosopher. Certain questions are so old that they cannot grow any older; they are susceptible only—and very concretely—to *another history*.

"Only language reveals, at the limit, the sovereign moment when it no longer has any currency. But in the end the one who speaks owns up to his impotence."[13]

§ 2 All the Rest Is Literature

The misfortune of a dreadful style in writing has befallen more than one philosopher—perhaps all of them.[1] It's a well-known fact, so well known that when the opportunity presents itself, it is truer to deem that it is not an accident, but rather an infirmity that is cosubstantial with and congenital to the exercise of philosophy. However, this can be understood in two ways: first, that this exercise condemns one to this infirmity; or, second, that this infirmity dooms one to this exercise. (However one chooses to look at it in the end, it is certainly about infirmity that one has to speak here, just as Kant did.) There is no lack, incidentally, of explanations and even excuses for this infirmity within and outside the body of the profession. The depth, the elevation, the complexity, or the gravity of philosophical thought tolerates if not demands some amount of dense writing. Indeed, it is not a little strange that this is the case up to a point where such a density not only spoils the charms of discourse but also perturbs its pure and simple legibility. The philosopher writes badly, and sometimes he or she does nothing but scribble.

At least that's the folklore of philosophical cacography. But it is evident that, in order to animate this lore, one must already possess in advance the aesthetic and literary categories that enable one to assess a style, or a lack or absence of it. In other words, one has to be in possession of *literature*. Literature can, in effect, either well subordinate philosophy to itself as a genre and bring to bear on it the only kind of judgment that does not arise from philosophical decision, or it can altogether exclude philosophy from its domain, from style.[2] But in order to make use of this notion of literature, and in order to delineate either of these partitions [*partages*], one needs philosophy. That is to say, the question of style, of the genre of philosophy—the question of how to present and expose philosophy, or, to say this in an absolute way, of philosophical exposition—must have been posed within philosophy itself. Since its most fully developed historical articulation was written in the German language, it is necessary to pose the question of Darstellung: Darstellung, ex-posing [*position-là*], in front of, exhibition, exposition, monstration [*monstration*], presentation, genre, or style.[3] And, insofar as no question can remain extrinsic, instrumental, or auxiliary to philosophy, it was necessary that this question be posed in philosophy as a philosophical question. It was necessary that this question be posed in such as way that it be philosophy, or perhaps be like philosophy, or the question *itself* of philosophy.

How to present philosophy? This question punctuates the history of philosophy with its repetitions. It punctuates—or syncopates?—it as a series of answers or affirmations. This is because philosophy, such and such a philosophy, is always a certain *how-to* of presentation and of its own exposition, an orthography: "And they would erase one touch or stroke and paint it another until in the measure of the possible they had made the characters of men pleasing and dear to God as may be. That at any rate would be the fairest painting (*graphê*)."[4] But there is a moment when this question *takes place* as a question, undertakes itself as a question, and begins to establish and articulate itself, thereby producing its own terms. This is the moment in which philosophy explicitly designates its own exposition as *literature*. That is to say, no longer as the trace of the very hand of the philosopher, his autograph, but rather as his other, that is . . . as all the rest.

There thus occurs a moment wherein the philosophical autograph can no longer in some sense certify, authorize, or authenticate itself, but wherein philosophy designates, implicates, exhibits, and disavows itself under the genre of what will become very quickly the modern notion—and hence *external* to philosophy—of "literature." This is the moment of Kant. And our task here consists simply in trying to establish the following proposition: it is beginning with Kant that it became possible and necessary to expressly distinguish between philosophy and literature (hence the cutting off and coupling of concepts and terms, and the positing of the question).

> Those people who have made a profession of explaining Kant to us were either of the sort who lacked the capacity to gain an understanding of the subjects about which Kant has written for themselves; or else such people as only had the slight misfortune of understanding no one except themselves; or such as expressed themselves even more confusedly than he did. —Friedrich Schlegel, *Athanaeum Fragments*[5]

Yet, in a certain sense, it is only a question of posing the fact of this proposition, and on account of it, of interesting ourselves in the difficulties Kant experienced as a writer. If Kant is the worst writer in the history of philosophy—or if he is so considered to be—it is not by accident. His misfortune is not an accident; nor is it an empirical infirmity. Rather, it belongs *systematically* to the ensemble of gestures and theses that constitute critical philosophy as such. By way of a programmatic formula that the rest of this book will have to verify, we shall propose the following: *the syncope of the autograph is constitutive of the whole of critical philosophy as such.* In other words, the whole wherein is decided and undecided, the last moment of metaphysics, our moment—insofar as we still have a "moment" to live or to occupy.

However, it will be a question here of Kant the writer. We are not about to embark on an examination of critical philosophy. Rather, we will set out to encounter it by way of a certain literary "crisis" in Kant and to establish such a "crisis" as a philosophical fact, or, as the philologists say, to establish the text.

The heavy, buckram style of Kant's chief work has been the source of much mischief; for brainless imitators aped him in his external form, and hence arose amongst us the superstition that no one can be a philosopher who writes well. —Heine, *Religion and Philosophy in Germany*[6]

The style of his metaphysical analysis is complicated, laborious, redundant, and often the harder the author worked to write clearly the more obscure was the result. The work of Kant is a thought in search of its form. If it were more finished, would it have been as exciting? —Boutroux, *La Grande Encyclopédie*

The strange blindness of all those who have bound Kant to the pillory of literature lies in the fact that they have never taken into account the statements of Kant himself, who never ceased to complain of lacking literary talent. And it goes without saying that philosophers, for their part, have considered his declarations even less. It is these that one must first attempt to read. We will read the repetition of this motif in the text of critical philosophy. "Why do I write such bad books" and "why do I wish to write good books."[7] This motif will reveal another one, which is also double: "In truth, says philosophy, there is only me—all the rest is literature," and "My truth, says the philosopher, can it do without the rest?"

(At the same time, in addition to certain marks that Kant's *writing* has left in philosophy, we shall reproduce along the way some of the traces that the same Kant has been found to have left, by means of a destiny unique amongst philosophers, in literature. No other philosopher, in fact, has taken on or left such an imprint beyond philosophy, whereas philosophers or critics furiously go at and exhaust themselves over his style. Immanuel Kant, one popular hero, regularly haunts high and low literature alike. What haunts novels, poetry, and theater alike, of course, is an eponymous figure of philosophy, of a superhuman virtue, for example, and of a science that the average mortal can barely understand. As

if literature could not do without it. But it is also the no-less-epon-
ymous figure of a certain ridiculousness of the philosopher, as if
literature, or even philosophy, could do without laughing. Everything occurs, in any case, as if it were inevitable that the failure of
Kant the writer marked the singular commencement of a singular
literary fortune and misfortune. Or, rather, as if Kant's literature,
in producing and completing the philosophical imparting [*partage*] of philosophy and literature, had at the same time, imprinted
on literature the indelible mark of its provenance.)

("At the same time, we will reproduce along the way . . . "—
Which "at the same time" is it a question of here? And of which
"way"? Will these texts, together with mine, come together to
form a unified text? Or will they be attached or glued to the side
of the road along the way? And on the way to where, since in a
certain manner, we are only on our way to these very texts, to
the nonautograph texts of Kant? The road and its edge are poorly
distinguished one from the other. There's something—or someone—here that is undecidable, a "*Kant Travestied*," just as there
have been Homers and Virgils *travestis* in literature; but wouldn't
the parody itself here be always very decidable. . . .)

All men, from the most austere to the most
frivolous, from the richest to the poorest, all
pursue, consciously or not, the same goal.
Even Kant? Probably even Kant, at bottom.
Even Lenin? I swear, in taking some time to
discover it, one would show that it is the case
even for him. —C. Fruttero and F. Lucentini,
Sunday Woman[8]

His style of conversation was popular in the
highest degree, and unscholastic; so much so,
that any stranger who should have studied his
works, and been unacquainted with his person, would have found it difficult to believe,
that in this delightful companion he saw the
profound author of the Transcendental Philosophy. —Thomas De Quincey, "The Last
Days of Immanuel Kant"

§ 3   A Vulnerable Presentation and a Desirable Elegance

—*Kant*: or cant as intelligible character."
Nietzsche, *The Twilight of the Idols*.[1]—(*cant*
originally implies the *jargon* of those who
put on the airs of the highest moral character.—Kant's father, in order to bear witness
to his Scottish origins, spelled his name Cant.
Immanuel chose the K in order to avoid the
pronunciation Zant. Zant means nothing;
neither does Kant. Is it possible that Immanuel applied the following rule from Du-
clos' *Grammaire*, which was intended for the
French: "The *K* is the letter we use the least
but which we should use the most, given that
it has no incorrect use"? Or did he remember
that *kant* was an old form of the past participle of *kennen*, to know?)

The presentation of philosophy is fragile, always in danger of
not being up to the task of the necessary exposition. The scope
and urgency of philosophical tasks needing to be carried out has
aggravated this fragility. The author himself, moreover, lacks the
gifts needed for the turn of phrase that would give it the necessary finish. And age, which continues to deplete his powers, leaves
him even less free time to chisel his forms: such is, in more than

one form, the motif that can be found scattered throughout Kant's texts, prefaces, notes, or announcements.

In order to account for it, at least in general, let us begin with some points of reference. It is first of all, in 1755, a deliberate gesture in the preliminary argument of Kant's *Nova dilucidatio*: "I have thus carefully avoided extensive digressions and only laid bare the muscles and joints of my argument, having put aside all charm and grace of language, like a discarded garment."[2] One discovers this gesture also in 1763, in the foreword of *The Only Possible Argument in Support of a Demonstration of the Existence of God*: "Because a variety of commitments have prevented me from devoting the necessary time to it, the manner in which these observations are presented shows the characteristic mark of something incompletely worked out. . . . In my case, the incomplete form of the work is to be attributed less to negligence than to deliberate omission. My sole intention has been to sketch the rough outlines of a main draft."[3] (Notice that the two reasons given here are inconsistent.) "It is my belief that an edifice of mean excellence could be erected on the basis of that draft, provided that hands more practiced than my own were to give it greater accuracy in the parts and perfected regularity of the whole."[4] (Another inconsistency. This time, the statement suggests not a voluntary gesture on Kant's part, but rather a failure of his own hand.) In 1764, the final note to the *Inquiry Concerning the Distinctness of the Principles of Natural Theology and Morality* attributes the lack of "refinement" in the text to a need to meet the deadlines of the Academy, but it adds that it will be easy to remedy this flaw afterward. The same year, in the *Observations on the Feeling of the Beautiful and the Sublime*, Kant excuses the weakness of his presentation of human failings: "For he to whom Hogarth's engraving stylus is wanting must compensate by description for what the drawing lacks in expression."[5]

(The first presentation in history of critical philosophy is not the *Critique of Pure Reason*, but rather a novel by Hippel, *Rising Careers*, which appeared between 1778 and 1780, and the hero of which takes a philosophy exami-

nation at the University of Königsberg. What
is more, Kant was suspected of being the true
author of the novel, or, at the very least, of
certain passages. He had to publicly deny it.
The episode of the examination permits the
reader to recognize big motifs of the *Critique*
then in preparation. For example: "Metaphysics has no relation to the senses. In it, everything is ordered on the basis of the mind. It is
a lexicon of pure reason, an attempt to bring
to light the propositions of pure thought.
What judgments are to logic, concepts are to
ontology, the concepts under which we place
things, *certificates* of understanding, *contained*
in reason. Metaphysics must be critical. Its
use is negative if—

"We were on the verge of setting off from
metaphysics with our eyes brimming with
metaphysics, but all of a sudden, *voilà!* We noticed the nightcap of her spectacular dignity,
the grandmother, who was obstructing the
doorway."

In 1783, the *Prologomena to the Metaphysics of Morals* will contain a series of remarks on the difficulties proper to philosophical
exposition. We will have opportunities to examine these later. The
preface to the 1786 *Metaphysical Foundations of Natural Science*
ends on the flaw of another genre that is supposedly also perfect:
"In this treatise, although I have not followed the mathematical
method with thoroughgoing rigor (which would have required
more time than I had to spend thereon), I have nonetheless imitated that method—not in order to obtain a better reception of
the treatise, through an ostentatious display of exactitude, but
rather because I believe that such a system is certainly capable of
this rigor, and also that such perfection can certainly be reached in
time by a more adept hand. . . . "[6] (Another accumulation of heterogeneous arguments: time and ability, but beyond that, we shall
soon see, that the mathematical perfection of philosophy is by no

means a matter of time and talent in execution.) The preface to the 1788 *Critique of Practical Reason* contains a defense against the accusation of having introduced a new and obscure language into philosophy. We shall have to return to it. As for the preface of the *Critique of Judgment* (1790), it asks for the reader's indulgence of the work, insofar as he expects to find therein a doctrine of taste, since that is not its intent. The preface continues: "Given how difficult it is to solve a problem that nature has made so involved, I hope to be excused if my solution contains a certain amount of obscurity, not altogether avoidable, as long as I have established clearly enough that the principle has been stated correctly" (*CJ*, 7). Allow us to add that in 1788, in the text entitled *On the Use of Teleological Principles in Philosophy*, Kant expresses his gratitude for Reinhold's *Letters on the Kantian Philosophy* in the following manner: "The talent of a luminous, even graceful presentation of dry, abstract doctrines without the loss of their thoroughness is so rare (at least in this age) and nevertheless so useful—I do not want to say merely for recommendation, but instead for the clarity of insight, of comprehensibility, and thereby of persuasion—that I feel obliged to publicly give thanks to the man who so complemented my work with this *clarification*, something I could not provide."[7] (One can thus see a continuous series of comments here link the very intelligibility of ideas to the lucidity of the text that presents them, and even—though how does this "even" function?—to the charms of this text. In the face of this concatenation, or inside it, how does one situate Kant's "infirmity"?)

The references can be multiplied without much difficulty.[8] But the preceding list of examples should suffice to evoke—it's the least that one can say—the insistence of this motif, as well as the diversity of the facets of Kant's work that it covers, often in contradictory ways. This diversity is gathered and organized—up to a certain point—by a text that may be considered as the matrix, or the accomplishment of all the others. This decisive text, which we have yet to cite, figures in the second preface to the *Critique of Pure Reason*; in other words, the distribution of this motif is not at all random. We will have to stop to consider this text.

Kant rarely composes and never characterizes
anything. But he always *wants* to do both.—
The Ideal of Confusion.—A choir of chaos
in Kant.—But at least with him confusion
needs composing. It's the first artistic chaos in
philosophy. —Friedrich Schlegel, *Posthumous
Fragments*

> Kant turns speculation into a useful, and even
> poetic, tool. —Novalis, fragment

Before taking on this text, however, we still need to first establish several points of reference. This is because the second preface
makes explicit and radicalizes a problem that was already posed in
the first preface of the *Critique of Pure Reason*, published in 1781.
On August 16, 1783, however, Kant writes to Mendelssohn:

> For although the book is the product of
> nearly twelve years of reflection, I completed
> it hastily, in perhaps four or five months, with
> the greatest attentiveness to its content but
> less care about its style and ease of compre-
> hension. Even now I think my decision was
> correct, for otherwise, if I had delayed further
> in order to make the book more popular, it
> would probably have remained unfinished. As
> it is, the weaknesses can be remedied little by
> little, once the work is there in rough form.
> For I am now too old to devote uninterrupted
> effort both to completing a work and also to
> the rounding, smoothing, and lubricating of
> each of its parts. . . . For an author who has
> projected himself into a system and become
> comfortable with its concepts cannot always
> guess what might be obscure or indefinite or
> inadequately demonstrated to the reader. Few
> are the men so fortunate as to be able to think
> for themselves and at the same time be able
> to put themselves into someone else's position

and adjust their style exactly to his requirements. There is only one Mendelssohn.[9]

"Think for oneself and, at the same time, from the point of
view of others": this formula—which combines the same and the
other, which thinks or demands the simultaneity of the same and
other—characterizes, since eighteenth-century German aesthetics
and especially since Baumgarten, the judgment of taste, as well
as the capacities that belong to the artist. Kant will transform its
empirical value into a transcendental determination by way of the
judgment of taste's "pretension to universality" in the *Critique of
Judgment*.[10] What the first *Critique* is lacking is being simultaneously the same and the other, is being a work of art—or at least
like a work of art, so that it may be able to claim the latter's universal communicability. But this lack, at the same time, is almost
nothing: it affects—beside Immanuel Kant himself, disappointed
by all the readers that the first edition of the *Critique of Pure Reason* put off—only the surface or the "movement" of the work. And
one can remedy the situation without much difficulty—although
Kant, here as elsewhere, gives precious few details on possible remedies, puts off the exercise to an unspecified future date, and ends
on a barely concealed appeal to the goodwill of the talented Mendelssohn. . . .

The second edition could have been an opportunity to apply
these remedies, or to compete with Mendelssohn. In fact (in this
regard) it will be the occasion of the second preface, wherein, instead of amending it, Kant will go on to repeat, specify, and, if one
may be permitted to say in the following way, aggregate the flaw
that only four years before he had characterized as accidental and
provisional to the very content of the work.

This repetition is itself preceded by the justification of a certain
obscurity or difficulty in expression necessary to the enterprise of
"speculative philosophy." This justification—which swears to a certain lack of popularity that we shall come back to—is itself taken
over from the first preface of 1781. The latter distinguished, in effect, "the *discursive* (logical) *distinctness* ARISING THROUGH

CONCEPTS" [*sic*] and "*intuitive (aesthetic) distinctness* ARISING THROUGH INTUITIONS" [*sic*] in order to explain that the author of the work, having considered the size of his work, had renounced the latter. That is to say, he had renounced "examples and illustrations" "that are necessary only from a popular point of view" (*CPR*, 11–12). We shall only remark in passing the fact that this distinction between two clarities implies a separation between the point of view of the concept and the point of view of intuition; this separation, the terms of which Kant underlines, is somewhat surprising given that only the combination of the concept and the intuition permits the production of a "signification." Doubtless, the "intuitive clarity" that Kant seems to exclude seems to derive from the domain of *empirical* intuition, whereas the intuition in the schema is a priori. But in this case, one can grant only one of the following two propositions: either the *Critique* presents itself by means of the clarity of concepts, though concepts without an a priori intuition are, as is well known, empty; or, the *Critique* presents itself by means of an a priori synthesis of the concept and the a priori intuition. This means that either the *Critique* is empty, or that it presupposes, for the sake of its own presentation, the a priori synthesis of the schema, the production of which has to be the content of this presentation. Which would open, in turn, a second set of alternatives: either the presentation and the content of the *Critique* are perfectly extrinsic to one another, or the solution to the theoretical problem of the *Critique* (synthesis) is furnished by its presentation rather than by its thesis. We shall see that such hypotheses will lead to dead ends with Kantian rigor. However, by the same token, we shall see that there can be no question of substituting in their place another possibility. This knot of questions already forms the undecidability of the *Critique of Pure Reason* as a book of philosophy.

But the undecidable does not allow itself to be circumscribed so quickly and so directly. Before witnessing the questions we have just evoked resurface in their own time, let us be content with retaining the following: the notion of popularity, and the agreeableness that it possesses, is not suited to the *Critique*: "Though always agreeable," writes Kant, "[it] might here even have had consequences running counter to my purposes" (*CPR*, 12).

The second preface twice repeats this motif. Critique "can never become popular" and must therefore "be carried out dogmatically and systematically according to the strictest demand, and hence carried out in a way that complies with academic standards (rather than in a popular way)" (*CPR*, 34). However, between the "popularity" excluded on principle and the obscurity of the first draft of 1781, there is, if you will, a certain margin: that of improvement and remedy. This second edition is also an occasion for clarifications, which, incidentally, have no impact whatsoever on the system, which Kant furthermore hopes "will continue to maintain itself in this unchangeable state" (*CPR*, 36). And if "much remains to be done as regards the [manner of] exposition," it is essentially a matter of "misunderstandings" the principles of which Kant has identified and which he enumerates (*CPR*, 36).[11] But he was unable to once again take up the revision of the entire book "because there was not enough time" (*CPR*, 36). By way of this transition, Kant introduces the figure of the reader on the last page of the preface, where he will—in a dubious continuity at least with the material that directly precedes it—hope and call for a new version and for access to popularity for the *Critique*.

> I have been pleased and gratified by what I have seen in various published writings . . . that the spirit of thoroughness in Germany has not faded away, but has only been drowned out for a short time by the tone in vogue, whereby people employ in their thinking a freedom that befits [only] a genius. And I saw that courageous and bright minds have gained mastery of my *Critique* despite its thorny paths—paths that lead to a science of pure reason which complies with school standards, but which as such is the only science that lasts, and hence is exceedingly necessary. These worthy men have

that happy combination of thorough insight with a talent for lucid exposition (the very talent that I am not aware of in myself), and I leave it to them to perfect my treatment of the material, which here and there may still be deficient as regards lucidity of exposition. For although there is in this case no danger of my being refuted, there certainly is a danger of my not being understood. . . . In the course of these labors, I have advanced considerably in age (this month I reach my sixty-fourth year). I must therefore spend my time frugally. . . . Hence I must rely on the help of those worthy men who have made this work their own, expecting them to clear up the obscurities in it that could hardly have been avoided initially, as well as to defend it as a whole. Any philosophical treatise can be tweaked in individual places (for it cannot come forward in all the armor worn by mathematical treatises), while yet the structure of the system, considered as a unity, is not in the slightest danger. Few people have the intellectual agility to survey such a system when it is new, but fewer still have the inclination to do so, because they find all innovation inconvenient. . . . Moreover, if a theory is internally stable, then any action and reaction that initially portend great danger will in time serve only to smooth away the theory's unevennesses, and in a short time they will even provide the theory with the requisite elegance, if those who deal with it are men of impartiality, insight, and true popularity. (*CPR*, 39–40)[12]

By way of its position and its tenor, this page circumscribes the whole of the question we shall explore here. We have to do little more than to write its commentary.

~

This commentary will begin by attacking this page at the weak point in the *armor* it was written to show off. A breastplate, let it be said in passing, that may very well resemble the one that must be worn by the valorous yet unhappy champions of the metaphysical tournament—the famous metaphor of the *Kampfplatz*, which is repeated in both prefaces—and whose victory it has never guaranteed.[13] A dress-armor more than a combat armor, more elegant than solid, and worn for the benefit of metaphysics, "the noble lady" of the *Critique of Pure Reason*.—Here, outside the Kampfplatz (since critique puts an end to these jousts), one nonetheless needs a suit of armor. Or, rather, we should say that if "the system" as such withdraws from the Kampfplatz, the "presentation" (the *Vortrag*, that which one brings forward, that which is ex-posed; several senses of this word are very close to those of Darstellung: execution, interpretation, and so on) is, for its part, still caught in it. Unless the last champion, Kant himself, having won the battle precisely by renouncing the rules and armor of the tournament, finds himself naked in the presence of the lady and does not feel the need for a new set of clothing. Because "how much wit [*Witz*] has been wasted in throwing a thin veil over that which, though indeed liked, nevertheless still reveals such a close relationship with the common species of animals that it calls for modesty?" (*A*, 25). Whether it is because he undressed his concepts or because he has exhibited his animality (would these amount to being the same thing? . . .), the philosopher, if he is no longer obliged to clad himself in armor, must still at least dress himself. And in this case, if, as the same passage from the *Anthropology* states, "The clothing makes the man," would the light armor of the tournament produce the transcendental philosopher?

However you look at it, the presentation is vulnerable because it is philosophical. This implies three things:

—first, that the presentation is not entirely independent of, nor even entirely heterogeneous, to the "content";

—second, to the extent that it presents itself, philosophy reveals a particular fragility;

—third, and as both the principle and the outcome of the first two statements, that philosophy cannot avoid going through this vulnerable exposition and exposing itself to blows.

Kant will never thematize this triple necessity on its own terms. It will always have the marginal, accidental, biographical, and provisional look that one can see here. It will always be the problem of Kant the writer and not of Kant's philosophy. Yet, its final result or its most general form, and, at the same time, the most faithful to what Kant will write, is manifestly *precisely what implicates Kant as a writer in his philosophy*. And which excludes him by implicating him, or more precisely what bothers, hurts, or wounds him.

> Nations who have sensibility do not have aesthetics. It's comical to see Kant, who must have had a dog's taste, in search of the beautiful.
>
> Nothing less artistic. *He did not know how to express himself.* Perhaps this universalist, having sensibility, desires intellectual power.
>
> A horrible simplification in Kant. —Paul Valéry, *Notebooks*

The only invulnerable presentation is mathematical presentation. It is a question neither of a more or less arbitrary example nor of a difference posited in relation to the outside of philosophy. This parenthesis in the preface, in fact, corresponds to *the most intrinsic* partition undertaken by the *Critique*; that is to say, it corresponds in one sense to *critique* itself. Mathematics is, in effect, the only adequate grammar [*régime*] of a joint presentation of the concept and the intuition that responds to it. It is thus the only locus of a *presentation*—of Darstellung—in the full and proper sense of the term. This is not the place to envisage the theoretical stakes of this determination—incalculable no doubt—which commands schematism itself, its whole game, and all its consequences. But we will hold onto the following: the partition of mathematics and philosophy opens the divide in Darstellung itself, the *crisis*, which *stricto sensu* separates Darstellung from another mode of "presentation," the philosophical one, which Kant specifically chose to call *Exposition*. In the first section of the "Discipline of Pure Reason" of the first *Critique*, Kant reminds us:

> *Philosophical* cognition is *rational cognition from concepts. Mathematical* cognition is rational cognition from the *construction* of concepts. But *to construct* a concept means to exhibit (darstellen) a priori the intuition corresponding to it. (*CPR*, 668)

The philosophical mode specifies the same text, is therefore the *discursive* mode, whereas the mathematical mode is *intuitive*; no element of mathematical procedure can ever "be imitated by the other" (*CPR*, 678). The first of these, "definition," means "to exhibit a thing's comprehensive concept originally within its bounds," but "only mathematics has definitions," and for philosophy, "instead of the term *definition*, I would rather use *exposition*," a term that is "more modest" (*CPR*, 680–81). *Discourse*, therefore, is the proper order of philosophy, and it is instituted by the fainting of original construction and presentation. Discourse arises out of the syncope of intuition and supplements it in the mode of exposition. (*Exposition*: in Latin or German, it's the same word as Darstellung, or the Vor-trag; it's *nearly the same*, so much so that one can believe it's not worth talking about; yet, all discursivity is obtained from this "nearly the same," in this undecided identity.)

The "modesty" of exposition is not limited to the realm of methodology. It points essentially to the most fundamental "modesty" of transcendental philosophy, the "modesty" that constitutes it *as* transcendental philosophy. Since one reads in the section entitled "On the Basis of the Distinction of All Objects As Such into Phenomena and Noumena" that "Its principles [those of the Transcendental Analytic] are merely rules for the exposition of appearances; and the proud name of an ontology . . . must give way to the modest name of a mere analytic of pure understanding" (*CPR*,

311). Exposition, that is to say, discourse—and discourse to the extent that presentation is impossible for it, thus necessarily belongs to Kantian phenomenality as such. The first preface that we earlier recalled had thus already, by the pretext or in the form of a simple setting aside of examples, *excluded* the exhibition [*présentation*] of the presentation [*l'exposé*] of Critique. The second insists on this determination of presentation [*l'exposé*] by exposition [*exposition*]. Philosophy as such is destined not to present itself "directly" (another determination that often characterizes Darstellung). And it is because it is condemned to this weakness—called discourse—that it must desire elegance.[14]

(Transcendental) philosophy thus does not define itself in any way in relation to literature. It defines itself—or rather *presents* itself—by a relation of exclusion from mathematical construction. At this stage, literature does not figure anywhere. It will ever only be—if it is ever anything more than the name of a problem—what philosophy tries to give itself in order to clothe itself, or at the least to compensate for the weakness of its armor. It will be a look, a writing, a style intended to palliate discourse. Palliate here means to replace, rectify, but always in an artificial, disguised way. To palliate [*pallier*] is to cover with a *pallium*, a coat—which can never serve as armor.

~

> How short-winded even the deeds of Napoleon look beside those of the pharaohs, the work of Kant beside that of Buddha, that of Goethe beside Homer! —Robert Musil, *The Man Without Qualities*

We have read that elegance is a matter of talent. "By talent (natural gift) we understand that excellence of the cognitive faculty which depends not on instruction but on the subject's natural predisposition. These talents are *productive wit* (*ingenium strictius sive materialiter dictum*), *sagacity*, and *originality* of thought (genius)," states §54 of the *Anthropology* (*A*, 115). Let us not trace right away the network of concepts and texts that this definition opens out on. We shall find them all in good time. The "talent of lucid presentation" can, in its indeterminacy, arise from three kinds of talent that Kant enumerates, and whose differentiation, moreover, is delicate at the very least from the moment one follows the text beyond this definition. There is thus in "talent" an excellence or a general eminence of the faculty of knowledge, an *acme* of reason—which doesn't necessarily mean a rational acme (reason is itself, in this section of the *Anthropology*, crowned by the analysis of talent, the highest of the "higher faculties of knowledge"). In this regard, it is hard to see how the *Critique of Pure Reason* and its author can lack talent without lacking . . . its object. Kant writes, though, that he lacks talent, at least "literary" talent. However, he also writes, it's true, that he is too old, or that the beginning of the project made it inevitable that there be some rough spots. Thus by his own admission, he doesn't simply lack talent. Either there remains more in this "admission" to decipher—or, rather, in these multiple and mixed-up "admissions."

> . . . come to close up the season of youth: my brain performed its functions as healthily as ever before: I read Kant again; and again I understood him, or fancied that I did. Again my feelings of pleasure, favorable for work and for the exercise of fraternity expanded themselves—poor words to translate the untranslatable—all around me. —Thomas De Quincey, *Confessions of an Opium-Eater*[15]

Kant does not lack talent. This proposition can be verified to be both a historical, anecdotal affirmation and a theorem of transcendental philosophy. It can be authenticated, as it were, by a double signature belonging to Kant; moreover, as we shall see, this amounts to imputing to this proposition simultaneously the sign of truth and of undecidability.

Let us begin with the theorem: it proceeds from the position and the nature that the *Critique* confers on *judgment*. Judgment, the object of the *Analytic of Principles*, the place and the operation of synthesis, constitutes the master articulation of the process of knowledge. However, the introduction to this *Analytic* starts off by positing judgment in general as having all the characteristics of what, in the *Anthropology*, is called talent: " . . . the power of judgment is a particular talent that cannot be at all learned but can only be practiced. This is also the reason why the power of judgment is the specific [feature] of so-called mother wit [*Mutterwitz*], for whose lack no school can compensate" (*CPR*, 206). *Mutterwitz*, maternal Witz—in the way that one says "mother tongue"— is the matrix of Witz in the *Anthropology*, of the talented mind, whose natural, original essence is thus underlined. One must immediately point out that Kant is dealing here with general logic, which is unable to give rules to judgment, before he goes on to introduce transcendental logic, "which seems to have as its proper business the task of rectifying and guaranteeing judgment according to rules."[16] Afterward, and above all, it is enough to read carefully what Kant writes about transcendental logic to discover that, although it proposes to "guarantee" judgment, it has no intention of teaching it itself. Transcendental logic consists rather in plunging itself into the "nature" of judgment, into its matrix—into the Mutterwitz—in order to grasp therein the principle itself of correctness, that is, of the limitation (to possible experience) of judgment *as "nature."* That is, in effect, what is produced from the very first chapter of the *Doctrine of Transcendental Judgment*, where *schematism* (the general procedure of judgment) is characterized in the famous sentence that it is necessary to reproduce here without, however, analyzing it:

> This schematism of our understanding [that is, its schematism regarding appearances and their mere form] is a secret art residing in the depths of the human soul, an art whose true stratagems we shall hardly ever divine from nature and lay bare before ourselves. (*CPR*, 214)

Having, if one may say, its matrix [*matrice*] in this deep womb [*matrice*], judgment is therefore a talent, or stems from talent (which doesn't mean that it's *nature* as a final instance, but rather that it can only be presented—or exhibited? or figured?—by way of an uncertain relation, at once of belonging and of contrast, to a "nature" understood as a abyssal depth, as mother, and also, if the "human soul" is in question here, as what will always escape a *psychologia rationalis* and could not arise from anything other than a *psychologia empirica*; the latter, however, can have no grasp on either the schema or a priori judgment). In other words, without talent, there can be no transcendental constitution of knowledge, but neither can there be one without a rectification, correction, and a surveillance of this talent—in itself however unassailable. Transcendental logic begins by renouncing the pure and simple spontaneity and the free and natural disposition of talent. It renounces what founds it and declares that it will regulate what escapes it. . . .

It is by means of an analogous gesture that Immanuel Kant became the author of the *Critique*. (Or could it be by way of the *same* gesture? But how could the history of the author and the production of the theory be the same thing? Unless by means of a vulgar and untenable reduction of one to the other? Not to mention that they are not the same thing—but their duality will not cease to pose the question of *another sameness*. . . .) In any case, for the moment let us say that one could take the risk of speaking of a "biographical theorem" contained in the admissions of the preface. In effect, Kant lacked talent so little that the "young" Kant, the one whom it had been possible to call the "elegant *Magister*,"[17] the one who in 1764 had been interviewed for a chair of eloquence and poetry, did not hurt his chances when he wrote for the occasion with all the talent one could hope for. As proof, we shall read the *Considerations on Optimism* of 1759 and, above all, *Dreams of a Spirit-seer Elucidated by Dreams of Metaphysics* of 1766, an essay full of verve, of Witz, of elegance, and of which the author who is (besides anonymous in 1766) very evidently a man of taste and spirit such as the fashion of the times (English and French, in this period, more so than German) could have desired.

> Given its subject-matter, it ought, so the author fondly hopes, to leave the reader completely satisfied: for the bulk of it he will not understand, parts of it he will not believe, and as for the rest—he will dismiss it with scornful laughter. —Kant, *Dreams of a Spirit-seer Elucidated by Dreams of Metaphysics*

The unhappy magister was spared nothing. At the very moment he was about to overtake the statue of Modesty, he heard a rustling sound that resembled that of a silk dress. Kant froze. From behind the statue of the goddess, he made out a stifled laugh. Something fell to the ground. Kant, with bated breath, took a half-step forward. At that moment, the moon came out from behind the clouds and illuminated with its cold light the face of a woman. It was Albertine. She was in the arms of a man who remained in the shadows. The head of the countess was thrown back, her mouth agape. Her svelte body pressed itself against that of the stranger. And when the man leaned slightly forward, the magister recognized the face of the Russian major in the moonlight.

Kant turned away. An indescribable horror rose in him. He quickly left the garden of the Palace of Keyserling. —Anton Treptow, *The Starry Sky Above Me: A Kant Novel*

Kant renounced his talent. In saying this, we don't mean to say that Kant renounced it "after 1766." We have already cited several texts prior to this date wherein he deplores his lack of elegance. It's not as a moment in a chronological series that this renunciation takes place, allowing one phase to succeed another, each clearly established in their identity. This renunciation takes place "somewhere"—a somewhere that is impossible to designate, and from where the same Kant, the author, the philosopher, undecides himself.—This renunciation is probably the first form we have encountered of a *decision* that orders philosophical discourse as such. It is not a decision taken by Immanuel Kant—and thus, strictly speaking, it is not a renunciation. Rather, it is something more like a *disappointment,* but on the condition that we understand that this disappointment does not happen to "Kant," and that, on the contrary, it constitutes him—and does so as a *disappointed identity.* If there is decision, it is, so to speak, of discourse itself. Through this decision, discourse chooses itself as discourse, gives itself the whole and explicit determination of discursivity. At the same time, it undecides itself because everything happens as if this determination, which is its *own,* did not entirely determine it, and it does so without remainder. It decides both discourse *and* the remainder, the remainder left over in discourse, the discourse-that-is-not-without-remainder.

～

In the years 1778–82—that is to say, either toward the end of the elaboration of the *Critique of Pure Reason,* or just after its publication—one finds in Kant's notes the following two mentions:

Mega biblion: mega kakon
1. System or rhapsody.
2. Elegance of the system.[18]

To distinguish the system from a rhapsody without order or principle is a constant concern for Kant (in the three *Critiques* inasmuch as in his *Logic*) because it is a transcendental requirement: the system is the unity that needs to be procured for the object, for knowledge, and for reason itself. And if *transcendental* means belonging to the order of a priori conditions of possibility, the condition of these conditions, if one may say so, is always the unity of the totality of a system.—However, everything unfolds as if, in order to conquer *critical* systematicity, one had to renounce elegance and to resign oneself to the *mega biblion*, that is to say, fall into the *mega kakon*. Yet everything unfolds also as if, once the system is put into place, one also *had* to consider its elegance . . . to dream of a *Critique* that is thin, svelte, wearing a silk dress. . . . Everything unfolds as if, at the very least, the renunciation gave rise to a desire that was equal to it—and a desire that takes root in all that was not accepted willingly (and could not be): the need to present the system itself simply and without graces. Because this presentation, this discursive exposition, is not a palliative—and, as a result, this palliative requires a palliative, one has to dress the coat.

(It is impossible to cite everything. Readers are thus begged to seek out on their own, for their instruction, the following works: Rudolph Gottschall, *Kant: A Poem*, 1849; August Schricker, *How Kant Ought to Have Married*, 1928; O. E. Hesse, *Symphony of Old Age*, stories based on Kant; Hermann Harder, *Kant and the Warbler*, 1933; and so on.)

Moreover, between the first and second prefaces, in 1783, Kant will have guarded against having lacked absolutely all grace. . . . In the *Prologomena to Any Future Metaphysics*, he writes, "If the reader complains about the toil and trouble that I shall give him with the solution to this problem, he need only make the attempt to solve it more easily himself. Perhaps he will then feel himself obliged to the one who has taken on a task of such profound inquiry for him, and will rather allow himself to express some amazement over the ease with which the solution could still be given, considering the nature of the matter" (*PFM*, 74). If a light touch (*Leichtigkeit, légèreté*) is not the same thing as elegance, at the very least the latter does not go without the former.

But there's more. These *Prologomena* are in fact already a palliative for a certain deficiency of the exposition of the first *Critique*; they are meant to "obviate the inconvenience" of "a certain obscurity arising in part from the scope of the outline." However, the simple (?) mission of a technical and economic palliative finds itself inextricably caught up in—just as all the motifs we are skimming here are simultaneously entangled, broken, and rejoined—other considerations, which overflow it. Between two editions of the *Critique of Pure Reason*, the *Prologomena* plead thematically and explicitly the cause of the difficulty of philosophical exposition and present themselves also as the "Prologomena to any future metaphysics that will be able to present itself *as a book*"; accordingly, it may be implied that hereafter there can no longer be a metaphysics that is not also, in fact and literally, but also literarily, its own book. It is enough here to skim Kant's book.

Edited for "future teachers," these prolegomena are meant "not to help them to organize the presentation of an already existing science, but to discover this science itself for the first time" (*PFM*, 53). They thus inscribe *critique* under the heading of an *ars inveniendi* that stems from a tradition received by Kant that intricately interweaves the requirements of logic and of aesthetics—or, to be more precise, corresponds to the emergence of what receives the name or names of *aesthetics*.[19] The aesthetics of *invention* is the intervention, in the order of discourse and knowledge, of a *je ne sais quoi*—sensible, affective, or artistic, which is the very condition of novelty. However, *critical* novelty constitutes, in relation to the metaphysical Kampfplatz, a radical philosophical exigency. This ars inveniendi will therefore have to consist first of all in a rereading of the *Critique* in a manner in which it can rethink it "in its entire extent and boundaries" (*PFM*, 58), a difficult requirement, but one which implies that Kant does not "expect to hear complaints from a philosopher regarding lack of popularity, entertainment, and ease, when the matter concerns the existence of highly prized knowledge that is indispensable to humanity, knowledge that cannot be constituted except according to the strictest rules of scholarly exactitude," because if "popularity may indeed come with time," it can nonetheless "never be there at the start" (*PFM*, 58). Thus, the scholastic exigencies of "science" are "excessively favorable to the cause itself," but "most certainly harmful to the work" (*PFM*, 58). "To invent," in metaphysics, is thus to choose science over the work, the school against genius, the content against the form. There is an "aesthetics" of the non-sensible, of the un-worked [*sans-œuvre*], or of the outside-the-work [*hors d'œuvre*]. Kant did not rest content with converting the aesthetics of the faculties of sensation into the science of a priori sensibility; he also constructs the conditions of an a priori aesthetics, one of the metaphysical *Opus*. The *Critique of Pure Reason* is the first philosophical *treatise* that conceives and determines itself as a "work," which means necessarily that it conceives of itself as a "work of art"—even if it does so negatively or problematically.

This is because things aren't so simple. After having so valiantly defended his cause, Kant nevertheless does not avoid, once again, the excuses and the accumulation of incongruous arguments.

> It is not given to everyone to write so subtly and yet also so alluringly as *David Hume*, or so profoundly and at the same time so elegantly as *Moses Mendelssohn*. . . .

Kant does not therefore have their talent, but still, he has something:

> But I could well have given my presentation popularity (as I flatter myself) if all I had wanted to do was to sketch a blueprint and commend its execution to others, and had I not taken to heart the well-being of the science that kept me occupied for so long. . . .

—And his renunciation is nothing other than a sacrifice:

> For after all it requires great perseverance and also indeed not a little self-denial to set aside the enticement of an earlier, favorable reception for the expectation of an admittedly later . . .

—although the sacrifice is not without benefit,

> but lasting approval. (*PFM*, 59 [translation
> modified])

—Trading on which Kant can conclude his introduction in a sort
of challenge tossed to those whose "talents" and "mental gifts" are
not up to the task of a metaphysical enterprise (*PFM*, 60).[20]

The *Prologomena* is haunted by the question of philosophical
presentation and its manner, a question that hereafter seems to
bifurcate: on the one hand, it is a question of a lack of elegance
to be acquired, and on the other hand, of the actual *invention* of
an exposition that would be proper to science. The philosopher
critic is like a stylist: he is the "very close relative" of the one who
"culls from a language rules for the actual use of words, and so to
compile the elements for a grammar" (*PFM*, 115). Grammar—the
discipline that Cartesian logic vainly attempted to appropriate (at
Port-Royal)—is a matter of usage, and thus of taste as much as of
reason. Critical philosophy is an inquiry into usage and taste carried out on reason with the intent of providing it with the rules for
its works. It is hardly astonishing if, just as every grammar would,
it poses the question of the usage and taste of the grammarian
himself and of his work. The critic and the grammarian always
go hand in hand in history, in line with a saying by Diderot that
can be read as the program of Kantianism: "When does one see
the birth of critics and grammarians? Just after the century of di-
vine productions and genius."[21] The critical grammarian poses the
question of the production of the œuvre to come: he is attached to
the (literary) work as if to something he himself has lost.

Just as the work of the *Prologomena* holds itself entirely, so to
speak, between the two remarkable appearances of the *book*—one
should write the *Book*—of philosophy. Until then, says §4, it does
not yet exist:

> One can point to no single book, as for in-
> stance one presents a *Euclid*, and say: "this is
> metaphysics." (*PFM*, 69)[22]

But it is important to understand that this book—impossible

to find and the name or title of which is confused with that of its author, or of which the signature has become the text if not the volume itself—nevertheless exists in some fashion, since Kant, in order to condemn the mistake of an adversary of the *Critique*, will use the following comparison in the final appendix:

> . . . just about as if someone who had never seen or heard anything of geometry were to find a Euclid, being asked to pass judgment on this book. . . . (*PFM*, 161)

Do we need to underline that Euclid—or the *Euclid*—is at the same time the paradigm or the paragon of mathematics (of geometry, that is to say, always the privileged example of mathematical Darstellung in Kant)? And is it necessary to listen to [*entendre*] what Kant—or what *Kant*—in silence, secretly (though just barely) understands, but does not hear [*entendre*]—what he wishes to hear [*entendre*]: here is a Kant, here is metaphysics.

The music of Kant: that I do not understand.
—Novalis, fragment

We are thus brought back to the partition between the philosophical and the mathematical . . . in the guise of their surreptitious identification. The renunciation of elegance and the critical position it forces Kant to occupy—or the reverse: the critical position and the renunciation of elegance it demands—repeats itself with a desire for elegance. Elegance is the term substituted for the presentation of the mathematical opus, and the desire for it is the desire to write a book. "Literature" will be the name of the object of desire of the lost opus.

Perhaps for the first time in philosophy (but there you have it: are we *inside* it? *How* can one be really inside it?)—at least for the first time in this form, and this formless assemblage of declarations—a philosopher wishes to be, *as a philosopher*, an author. Or philosophy obliges a philosopher to wish to be an author. And to designate, in advance, for posterity, his own name as the proper name of the philosophical Book—no one doubts that it must be of a grand style . . . —just as he designates, in retrospect, with a symmetrical gesture, a philosopher as a literary model—and specifically the philosopher David Hume, whom the new author completes in every sense of the word. (And one could here analyze another question [the same]: What is the relation between Humean empiricism and Hume's style in Kant's attitude toward the one who, as we know, "interrupted" his "dogmatic slumber"?)

All this, nevertheless, is not as decided as it may perhaps seem. Nothing here rests on rigorous concepts, nor on the strict delimitation of boundaries that makes up the nervous system of the *Critique*. At the same time, two perfectly heterogeneous entities are placed in relation to one another, but in an obscure, unexpected relation: philosophy and style, or elegance. And, at the same time, nothing allows one to distinguish literature, on the one hand, from philosophy, on the other.

The state of *jouissance* is not favorable to close study, and a tasteful treatment breaks the logical machinery, upon which all philosophical conviction is founded. Furthermore, Kant's *Critique of Pure Reason* would be manifestly more imperfect if it had been written with more taste. But a writer of this genre cannot expect to interest readers who do not share in his goals. —Friedrich Schiller, *Letter to Prince Holstein*, November 21, 1793

§ 4   The Ambiguity of the Popular and a Science Without Honey

Reverie à Königsberg.
Il se disait: "Plus tard . . . Kant, dira-t-on."
—Raymond Queneau, *Les Œuvres complètes de Sally Mara*[1]

It is still a question, in particular, of the impossibility or the danger of being "popular." In other words, of a notion or of an image that is in turn undecided. Popular philosophy is first of all specifically the one that Hume describes by opposing it to the speculative kind in the beginning of the *Enquiry Concerning Human Understanding*.[2] It is the philosophy of counsel, of example, and of exhortation—a moral discourse alongside a dogmatics. It is also, consequently, a rhetorical philosophy, or belongs to the rhetorician, alongside the "anatomy" practiced by the thinker.

For example, such is the talent of the "ingenious and eloquent" and "already renowned" Herder, whose *Ideas for a Philosophy of the History of Mankind* Kant reviewed in 1785. According to the latter, the former demonstrates "adroitness in unearthing analogies" and a "bold imagination" in "wielding" them, as well as the art of "equivocal hints which cool, critical examination would uncover in them."[3] Here, then, is a philosopher who writes happily, but here is a happiness that could be a conceptual lure. Popular style is analogy rather than demonstration, color rather than line. In "popular language" all is given "as mere probability, reasonable

46

conjecture, or analogy," by which "the naturalist of pure reason" "cloaks his ill-founded claims" (*PFM*, 107). It would suffice to re-read Leibniz's chapter on judgment—on judgment as *semblance of truth* [vrai-semblable] and as analogy—to understand that meta-physical idealism has a part of it bound, according to Kant, to the brilliant style of the popular genre, and that, consequently, the refusal of this style is a *critical* gesture in every sense of the word.

The stakes are in effect those of presentation. Because *color*, the art of which is always inferior to the point that painting precedes it as an art on the basis of drawing alone (*CJ*, §51), is what is not capable a priori of Darstellung: "Conical shape can indeed be made intuitive without any empirical aid, merely according to the concept of a cone; but the color of this cone will have to be given previously in some experience or other" (*CPR*, 670). The figures of the geometer are colorless; by the same token, the presentation of science, or of the system, according to a metaphor that is a constant of the *Critique*, must always be that of a *drawing*, a *tracing*, a *blueprint*, or an *outline*. The outline for the book of philosophy is not a technical restriction that lies outside its content: it is *reason* itself, and the Book should be entirely contained [*devrait tenir tout entier*] in its blueprint. But what happens when this blueprint can no longer be neither the ontologico-narrative order of the *Meta-physical Meditations*, nor the *more geometrico* order of the *Ethics*?[4] The philosopher asks himself the question of "popular color"— and one can well see what follows from the replacement of "ontol-ogy" with the "modest" title of "exposition": ontology engenders its own blueprint and its own book; exposition turns the problem of the fabrication of the blueprint, the creation of a drawing, into the "ontological" problem.

Next, just imagine a total universal order em-bracing all mankind—in short, the perfect state of civilian order: that, on my honor, is death by freezing, it's *rigor mortis*, a moon-scape, a geometric plague!

"I discussed that with my library attendant. He suggested that I read Kant or somebody,

all about the limits of ideas and perceptions.
But frankly, I don't want to go on reading."
—Robert Musil, *The Man Without Qualities*

As we saw, the popular style is style itself; it is eloquence or color in themselves. This style—or style as such—is moreover not unrelated to a certain poem, and even with the origin of poetry. This origin is none other than the priest. It's in effect through the exclusion of the priestly poem that *reason alone* traces the *boundaries* of *religion*: "That 'the world lieth in evil' is a complaint as old as history, even as old as the older part of poetic fiction; indeed, just as old as that oldest of all fictions, the religion of the priests" (*R*, 69).[5]

Yet this poem, this fiction [*Dichtung*] or this narrative is a popular one:

> For what is easier than to grab and to partake with others of a narrative made so accessible to the senses and so simple, or to repeat the words of mysteries when there is absolutely no necessity to attach any meaning to them! And how easily does this sort of thing find access everywhere, especially in conjunction with the promise of a great advantage, and how deeply rooted does faith in truth of such a narrative become when the latter bases itself, moreover, upon a document long recognized as authentic, and faith in it is thus certainly suited even to the commonest human capacities! (*R*, 199)

The popular thus has some part of it that is related to the origin of narrative, more original than history, as well as—since on this point more than perhaps any other regression is probably inevitable—with the narrative of the origin (the last passage cited above is directed explicitly at the Bible; would it be necessary to repeat, in another tone: Mega biblion: mega kakon?). The appeal of this narrative is clear, and the philosopher, so far as he's concerned, could not wish for better for the account he intends to give of the origin itself. Nevertheless, it is precisely the question of origin *itself* that critical philosophy intends to renounce. At the same time, it intends to renounce the prestige of popular narrative. Is the former the cause of the latter? We will never be able to say. However, as attractive as the popular may be, and perhaps *because* it is attractive, it happens to be the case that only common mortals are subjugated by narratives, mysteries, and priests. The popular is the heteronomy of reason.

> Kant . . . decorates skepticism with flourishes and scholastic frills in order to make it acceptable to the formal scientific taste of the Germans. . . . Not a single breath of cosmopolitical taste nor of classical beauty has yet grazed it [*effleurer*]. —Nietzsche, posthumous fragment

It is therefore still the autonomy of reason—the principle and condition of critique—that demands that the philosopher reject a popularity wherein reason, in the grip of sensibility, submits itself blindly to dogmatism. Moreover, moral autonomy is nothing other than that which simultaneously institutes the autonomous "tribunal" of theoretical reason and reemerges out of the judgment of this same tribunal. It's also why this tribunal, still the same one, prescribes by its decrees an ethic and a deontology of philosophical presentation. This deontology of presentation constitutes the "ontology" itself of pure reason. The preface of the first book of the *Metaphysics of Morals* firmly recalls it (as if, according to a new and different, and equally unavoidable reversion, the presentation of morality needed to be preceded by the morality of presentation). In question is "M. Garve," who would like to impose upon "all writers, but especially for philosophic writers" the "duty" of being "popular." He "rightly requires . . . that every philosophic teaching be capable of being made *popular* (that is, of being made sufficiently clear to the senses to be communicated to everyone) if the teacher is not to be suspected of being muddled in his own concepts" (*MM*, 366).

> I gladly admit this with the exception only of the systematic critique of the faculty of reason itself. . . . This [system] can never become popular . . . although its results can be made quite illuminating for the healthy reason (of an unwitting metaphysician). Popularity (common language) is out of the question here; on the contrary, scholastic *precision* must be insisted upon, even if this is censured as hair-splitting (since it is the *language of the schools*); for only by this means can precipitate reason be brought to understand itself, before making its dogmatic assertions. (*MM*, 366)

The *writer-philosopher* must therefore accept being unpopular, which, for all that, has nothing to do with sophistical pedantry, since, Kant continues: " . . . if *pedants* [*sic*] presume to address the public (from pulpits or in popular writings) in technical terms that belong only in the schools, the critical philosopher is no more responsible for that than the grammarian is for the folly of those who quibble over words (*logodaedalus*)" (*MM*, 366).[6] The language of the academy is *punctual*: its terms respond point by point to those of thought; it does not mix up the meaning of these terms or play with them, and although, by all evidence, the academy implies some artifice, or at least some absence of the natural, its language is not an artificial one. The philosopher is not and does not have the right to be a logodaedalus.

∿

Sober and scientific, the autonomy of reason presents and monitors itself within the autarchic circle of the school. Its end, however, and its reason, if one is permitted to say it in the following way, would not be attained if it could reach only students. Even so, as we have just stated, it is itself perfectly accessible "to sound reason (that of a metaphysician who doesn't know that he is one)"[7]—or, at least it is possible to render it perfectly clear to the man of the people whose "health" is without question the guarantee of spontaneous metaphysical ability. How can it be thus rendered—*gemacht*, made, fabricated? What know-how [*savoir-faire*] (that is not, however, a *logodaedalie*) must one use? This is what is not written here.

That is what the preface of the first *Critique* wanted to show, and what Kant seems to still be awaiting and promising the arrival of ten years later (we're in 1797): this clarity and this desirable elegance—which are also, let us not forget, palliatives, preservatives, and balms—to procure these for critical philosophy, there was a need for "men of impartiality, insight, and true popularity" (*CPR*, 40).

The *writer-philosopher* needs another person for his book. Who is he, this other? A writer? A philosopher? We know only that he must not be a logodaedalus. Let us wait a little longer to learn his name. But let us remark and hold onto the fact that he must be capable of "true popularity." There are, therefore, two popularities, or the popular is itself ambiguous. The deontology of presentation here encounters an ambiguity that involves, as we shall see, morality itself.

Morality comes, as we know, from common experience to the extent that it is an experience of the moral law inscribed at the bottom of every heart.[8] It is probably necessary, if one looks more closely, to understand here that "common" experience is common only to the extent that it is the experience of *pure* practical reason, and one should not confuse the *sensus communis* with the *sensus vulgaris*.[9] But at the same time, one must recall that pure reason is here in absolute need of its popular presentation for its demonstration. The criterion of "good faith" is a *fact* accessible to everyone, and to which the philosopher must be able to appeal in order to therein designate the *right*. The moral law—if we may be permitted to do without the requisite analyses—is in some sense essentially popular. That is why the preface to the *Critique of Practical Reason* can—and must—declare that "the kind of cognition itself approaches popularity" (*CprR*, 145). *Popularity* is no longer here a literary elegance that is more or less fallacious, but rather the thing itself of reason (because, in addition, one should not forget that moral "knowledge" is not pasted onto theoretical knowledge from the outside; it is prescribed and programmed *by* the latter and *for* itself. What is at stake in morality is the status of reason in general. As a result, therefore, it is all of a sudden in play in "popularity."). Moreover, *Religion* within its mere boundaries is itself "easily intelligible in lessons for children and in popular sermons."

> As you have already often noticed, Kant likes to ascribe philosophical meaning to passages of Scripture. It is quickly evident that for him it's hardly a matter of supporting the authority of Scripture, but rather of connecting the results of philosophical thought to the reason of children, and in this way, of popularizing them. —Friedrich Schiller, Letter to Gottfried Korner, February 28, 1793[10]

There is therefore a point at which reason *is* popular, instead of needing to have a *pallium* of popularity. But then why would it need a presentation that is, in spite of everything, scholastic, why does the *Religion Within the Boundaries of Mere Reason* use "expressions that are only for school." Ultimately, the deontology of presentation should reverse itself. If it does not do so, if, to the contrary, the philosophical enterprise regarding religion consists in rigorously separating biblical colors from the rational outline of Christianity, it is because moral popularity cannot be entirely separated from the ambiguity of the popular. And perhaps the thing itself—morality and religion—insofar as it is popular, remains dangerously ambiguous. The popularity of practical reason seems to lead back to, if not reinforce, the ethic of presentation as the morality of morality itself: it is the only thing that can prevent morality from reverting back into heteronomy, the calculation of merit, or superstition. And yet, it is moral autonomy itself, it is pure morality that is by itself, if one may risk saying it this way, *purely popular.* What is remarkable, however, is that nowhere does Kant propose the construction of a concept of the "purely popular"—no more so than of a concept of "pure elegance. . . . "

Where then is to be found the partition between true and false—between good and bad—popularity [*se partagent*]? Where does the *communis* distinguish itself from the *vulgaris*—an opposition that it is astonishing to see failing to function in a more constant and clearly axiological manner? One never quite knows very clearly. Rational popularity (*popularitas rationalis practica*, as Kant—or *Logodaedalus?*—could have, but did not write . . .) seems to inevitably dress itself in worldly popularity, and the mystery of this incarnation constitutes an obscure place where—with the help of the displacements of a word, "popularity," ceaselessly repeated—the crucifying rigor of philosophical presentation resolves itself [*se decide*].

> That's just the place for him! I told [Kant] that day at breakfast, "Say what you will, Professor, but you have thought up something that makes no sense. It may be clever, but it's altogether too abstruse. People will laugh at you." —Comment made by the Devil in *The Master and the Margarita*, Nicolas Bulgakov

In effect, it is the cross that is probably a necessary representation of the "prototype," by virtue of the obligatory recourse to "analogies" (by way of or for the purposes of popularity) such as that are manipulated by the "poet-philosopher" (*philosophischer Dichter*) Haller—and not only because of the "*example* of a human being well-pleasing to God" through his "conduct" and "suffering," that is to say, the Christ of the popular narrative (*R*, 106). Rather, it's the cross because Kant cannot decide on the true and moral exposition of reason except by offering the example of his own sacrifice, that is to say, except by renouncing to write like the "poet-philosopher." (This is the case, "even though we cannot form any concept through reason of how a self-sufficient being could sacrifice something that belongs to his blessedness, thus robbing himself of perfection" in the manner that Kant writes of Christ [*R*, 107].[11] Which implies only one of the following two consequences: either the philosopher is not sufficient unto himself and lacks the essential autonomy of reason; or, we can no longer conceive the philosopher except as the archetypal Christ.) As if it were impossible to truly separate the two popularities—to *delimit* them—one can only cross the motif of one with that of the other. But the chiasmus thus produced, the crossing of popularities, is a locus of confusion rather than a new distribution [*répartition*]. This is because renouncing one popularity renders the other undecided. Why and how do we require a presentation that is simultaneously lucid and scholastic? And, at the same time, one awakens and reawakens a desire for the other popularity.

~

However, can popularity still be understood—at bottom, there's nothing surprising about this—as a faculty that is entirely necessary and superior—as a *talent*, the talent of choosing, in fact, that is, of discerning . . . for example, between two popularities? A note dating from 1788 or the years 1790–1800 says, "The popularity of a refined and cultivated intellect is taste. . . . The aptitude of choosing in a popular manner is the absence of taste."[12] But another note, written between 1776–80, determines the superiority of this faculty in another, more precise (if one may say so), manner.

> Scholastic presentation and popular presentation. The latter is the work of a genius.[13]

The man of true popularity is a genius. This also means that *true* popularity can only be discerned and put to work by a genius. Let us not be in too much of a hurry to learn who this genius might be. He will present himself, moreover, and perhaps even on his own.—Let us rather return to the crucial decision in which the ethic of presentation is produced. We shall see that this decision is systematically related to a *critical* decision that engages philosophy as such.

It's a question, of course, of philosophy such as it has to be established by critique, that is, as we know, of the science of metaphysics as a science. However, science as such is not capable of being, in a general way, beautiful. It is an imperative (which probably
makes up the theoretical version of the categorical imperative) that
Kant decides about in the same gesture that puts an end—or that
he believes puts an end—to the aesthetic debates of the eighteenth
century: in the same way as "there is no science of the beautiful,
but only critique"; in the same way as:

> As for a fine science: a science that as a science
> is to be fine is an absurdity; for [treating it] as
> a science, we asked for reasons and proofs, we
> would be put off with tasteful phrases (*bons
> mots*). (*CJ*, 172)[14]

Beauty is incapable of the autodemonstration—of demonstrative autonomy—that science implies. Demonstrative autonomy
complete and whole, we know, belongs only to mathematics. Yet
mathematics, inaccessible, remains no less the rule and the model
of all scientific procedures. This can be formulated more precisely:
mathematics comprises an autodemonstration [*autodemonstration*] through and in an *automonstration* [automonstration] (the
visible *construction* of the concept in intuition); beauty comprises
an *automonstration* [automonstration] without autodemonstration
[*l'autodemonstration*]: beauty is thus banned in the same way that
mathematics is impossible.[15] In both cases, automonstration is the
element that is excluded, dangerous, or inaccessible to philosophy.
Autonomous demonstration remains, therefore, something of a
principle and a rule of exposition: that is to say, a kind of mathematics without beauty.

Moreover, if as we know, demonstration can attach itself to elegance, it is only with the reservation that "it would also be quite
improper to call it *intellectual beauty* . . . " (*CJ*, 243–44).[16] If it's
true that mathematics and beauty have in common the character
of autodemonstration, then this "community" as such remains indeterminable. There is automonstration and automonstration, just

as there is popularity and popularity. And because in both cases, it is hard to distinguish one from the other, one runs the greatest risk: the risk of a certain *disorientation*, as we shall see. (In passing, let us remark the following: all this "logic" implies perhaps that philosophy, in order to erect mathematics as a model—though it be inaccessible—must begin by clearly separating beauty and mathematics by denying that a certain "style" is inherent to mathematics, and that this belongs to the realm of art and, more precisely, to writing and *drawing*. All of which can probably only occur at the price of an arbitrary and violent gesture that the whole discourse of the philosopher works to camouflage. "Literature" will be the complex, mixed-up remainder of this violence, itself distressing.)

The aesthetic, inadmissible substitute for demonstration will be the *bon mot* (written in French in Kant's text, the word "*mot*" obviously points to the French *esprit* and to all its frivolity . . .). The bon mot is the Witz, and if it isn't entirely the Witz, this intellectual *talent*, it is in any case, the danger proper.[17] The Witz is always the threat of a certain disorder, of a certain superficial and obscure turn; the bon mot can be in bad taste (even though Kant hardly ever has recourse to this axiological argument: the distress of the Witz is too seductive for him to do that; the puritan condemnation of the Witz will be left for Hegel to carry out, by which we can see that the most moral one is not who we tend to think is . . .). In short, the Witz can always degenerate into a "bon mot," and the bon mot is by nature superficial, inconstant, and murky; it might even be *vulgar*:

> . . . a bright, dewy, vaginal laughter such as Jesus H. Christ and Immanuel Pussyfoot Kant never dreamed of, because if they had the world would not be what it is today and besides there would have been no Kant nor Christ almighty. —Henry Miller, *Tropic of Capricorn*

It's probably not inconceivable "that one has Witz along with profundity," but "profundity is not wit's business" (*A*, 117). Nothing prevents it from sometimes being "a vehicle or garb for reason." But it is precisely the veil that is ambiguous: it decorates it; it favors it, and it . . . veils. The veil is essentially improper (to the extent that one can speak of the essence of this borrowed faculty, absent from the canonical catalog of faculties but ceaselessly added or brought back or attached to the description of the superior faculties, without nevertheless its status therein ever being exactly decided). And if the Witz, turning back on itself the play of its own constitutive rhetoricity, justifies that one speak of a wit that is "*blooming*," it is on the condition that "nature seems to be carrying on more of a game with its flowers but a business with fruits . . ." (*A*, 96).[18]—Again, Witz has a right to this praise only on account of the description of the faculties. When it is a question of *forming* reason, of educating it, it is necessary to carefully inspect this Witz, which "does nothing but produce pure silliness if it's not combined with the faculty of judgment."[19]

However, it is the temptation of play, that is, an overly natural disposition for play that one must be able to set aside if one wishes to bring reason into its own as sound critique, if one thus wishes to safeguard science:

> Everyone will readily admit that a discipline is in many respects required for our temperament, as well as for those talents (such as imagination and ingenuity) that like to allow themselves free and unlimited movement. But that reason, which properly is obligated to prescribe its discipline to all other endeavors, itself needs a discipline—this may indeed seem strange. And reason has, in fact, thus far escaped such humiliation precisely because, given the solemnity and thorough propriety with which it deports itself, no one could easily have come to suspect it of playing frivolously with imaginings in place of concepts, and with words in place of things. (*CPR*, 666)

What is strange and unsettling, therefore, is not the Witz or the bon mot as such, it's their frivolity, which is housed within reason itself. One must prepare, correct, critique reason *itself* in order to achieve *reason itself*. This requirement, informative or reformative, ethical and aesthetic, constitutes at the same time the principle of the whole *Critique* and its most equivocal point: the locus of obscurity, that is, of the syncope of *purity itself*. In any case, it is the reason why science is necessary. The rigor of science consists in the fact that reason begins by inflicting the discipline of serious- ness and fruitful toil on itself. The ethics of presentation begins in the mortifying asceticism of the concept. This "need" in reason will not have sufficiently severe demands in order to be satisfied: already as a reader, and not only as a writer (how does one dis- tinguish between the two?), Kant must in effect sacrifice himself, renounce, repress, or kill something in himself:

> It is a burden for the understanding to have taste. I must read and reread Rousseau until the beauty of his expressions no longer dis- turbs me, and only then can I first investigate him with reason. (*NF*, 5 [translation modi- fied]) —Kant, *Remarks on the Observations of the Feelings of the Beautiful and the Sublime*

—It wasn't according to Kant, that's certain. Far from it.—That's a case either of logic carried into the blood or of stagnation. . . . —Andrey Biély, *Saint Petersburg*

Beauty, too—what is pleasing and what disturbs—is at best good only for the weak and for children. Science, by contrast, *must be* bitter:

> The aesthetic is only a means for accustoming people with too much tenderness to the rigor of proofs and explanations. As when someone rubs honey on the rim of a vessel for children. (*NF*, 529)

However, the moment one ceases to be a child, honey is useless, and even dangerous. To the extent that the *Critique* excludes aesthetic and popular exposition (but we know already that this "extent" still needs to be appreciated, if that is possible), the reader of the *Critique* is thus supposed to be an adult. This supposition does not go without saying, since reason, in submitting its own "frivolity" to critique, thus finds itself being simultaneously grown up and childish. One could think of an intermediate state, a puberty or an adolescence of reason. The *Critique*, however, is not a transition. It is a definitive establishment of boundaries. All transition is inconceivable for Critique; as a result, an inevitable coexistence, or copresence, of the adult and the juvenile, the frivolous and the serious, constitutes the *undecidability* itself of Critique, the undecidability of its sameness, or of what is, in the final analysis, Critique *itself*. This is *therefore* precisely what Kant must decide with the greatest intransigence.

Honey is forbidden. So when in 1787 the matter of translating the first *Critique* into Latin arose, Kant pointed out that the translator ought to be careful that its "style" not "aim too much at elegance," and suggested that it should be instead "more or less Scholastic" in order to ensure its "precision and correctness," even if one must thereby commit some abuses of correct classical Latin (*C*, 261).[20] But a rule of this kind applies to all intellectual activity. The problem of elegance is only a problem of form to the extent that thought itself is indissociable from its form. *In Critique, reason forms itself.* This expression must be understood in all its senses simultaneously. The scholastic rule against elegance, or the bitterness against honey, signifies thereby that one must prefer *brains*, such as Newton, who "could show this not only to himself but to everyone else as well," and whose talent as a scientist lies "in continuing to increase the perfection of our cognitions" over geniuses such as *Homer* or *Wieland*, whose "skill cannot be communicated" (*CJ*, 176–77). Moreover, the business of genius is art, and "art stops at some point, because a boundary is set for it beyond which it cannot go and which probably has long since been reached and cannot be extended further" (*CJ*, 177).[21]

Next to the helot was the bust of a thinker
with puckered brow, who wore an expression
of intense and fruitful meditation. On the
plinth was the name:
    IMMANUEL KANT
    . . . The magpie . . . with a few flaps of its
wings, reached the bust of Immanuel Kant;
on top of the stand, to the left, was a little
perch on which the bird landed.
    Immediately, a strong light illuminated the
skull from within, and the casing, which was
excessively thin, became completely transparent from the line of the eyebrows upwards.
    One divined the presence of countless re-
flectors placed facing in every direction inside the head. So great was the violence with
which the bright rays, representing the fires
of genius, escaped from their incandescent
source.
    Repeatedly the magpie took flight, to re-
turn immediately to its perch, thus constantly
extinguishing and relighting the cranial
dome, which alone burned with a thousand
lights, while the face, the ears and the nape
of the neck remained in darkness. Each time
the bird's weight was applied to the lever, it
seemed as though some transcendent idea
was born in the thinker's brain, and it blazed
suddenly with light. —Raymond Roussel,
Impressions of Africa

   This limit or this border (*Grenze*) imposed on art is the limit
inscribed at the highest moment of the analysis of aesthetic judgment, that is, in the analytic of the sublime. The judgment of the
sublime exhibits, as it were, a chasm between art and reason. In it,
we can only feel the inadequation between "the infinite in common reason's judgment," which is capable of thinking "a progres-
sively increasing numerical series," and our inability "to *grasp* the
infinite given in its entirety as a whole" (*CJ*, 111).[22] The sublime

consists in a radical inadequation between the aesthetic and the mathematical; thus, it reproduces and constrains the very position of philosophy. Critique is the analysis—vertiginous, syncopated— of the sublime fracture of Reason.

"Then we feel in our mind that we are aesthetically confined within bounds," and from this point of view "all aesthetic comprehension is small, and the object is apprehended as sublime with a pleasure that is possible only by means of a displeasure" (*CJ*, 117). Everything thus happens as if the compulsion at stake in the sublime had to, by means of the denunciation of the "pettiness" of art and the limits of its comprehension (*Zussammenfassung*: the *seizing-together*, the seizing of the same or in the same), come to exercise itself through the necessary substitution of science for art. The displeasure, the bitterness, the pain of science *is necessary*. The slow, graceless procedure of "mechanical intellects" is necessary—in the *Anthropology*, it is the name that is used to refer, at least in part, to the "brains" of the first *Critique*. Because "mechanical rules" are needed so that one can adapt "the product to the . . . *truth* in the presentation of the object that one is thinking of" (*A*, 120 [translation modified]). Genius would thus be madness, and *truth* demands a laborious science without style. It demands it in Darstellung, as if it were in the precise moment of presentation (posited here in its difference from simple and pure thought) that resided the specific danger and the trouble of aesthetic honey. It is only at this price that philosophy will be able to enjoy a pleasure that would no longer owe anything to this honey. Science demands a *jouissance* that is impassive.

I am unable to read the *Critique of Pure Reason* without feeling the most violent agitation. Every word in it, it seems to me, is incandescent, shot through with the frisson of the most profound, the most true, the most elementary feeling. No other poem seeking to communicate or the immediacy of feeling, except perhaps *Faust*, is able to produce an affective impression equal to the one I re-

ceive from this work, apparently glacial, of
pure thought. As strange as it may seem, the
Critique of Pure Reason is for me one of the
most passionate, indeed the most passionate,
of world literature. —Ernst Horneffer, *Pla-
tonism and Our Time*, 1920

The whole philosophical tradition, one must immediately add,
has said little more than this. The properly philosophical tradition
devoted to the subject of presentation and the Book of philosophy
even consists in saying it, in imposing on itself the ascetic mortifi-
cation that dissolves elegance in labor. In effect, Kant repeats this
tradition.

However, we can also see that in the Kantian repetition this imperative having to do with presentation presents itself, and it does
so in the very concepts of the doctrine as a necessity that belongs
to the structure and the essence of knowledge. This, too, is likely
part of the entire tradition, but right up until Kant, presentation's
belonging to science is always, in one way or another, thought in
terms of dependency or consequence. Form must demonstrate itself to be coherent with the content. The Kantian repetition of this
tradition consists in radicalizing this belonging, *in making form
itself the very stakes of the content*. (It is, moreover, too much or too
little to say "radicalize"; henceforth, we will not cease to "confirm"
that, in fact, every "radical" [or "root"—Trans.] collapses or dissolves in the undecidable form/content of philosophical science).
The effect—or, simultaneously the cause—of this "radicalization"
is that the knowledge to which presentation belongs is a knowledge that henceforth maintains a systematic, essential, and structural relation with art and the work of art. With the image (?) of
the armor and the finery of *elegance*, therefore, the preface to the
first *Critique* presents a problem of legibility that is also a problem of scientificity. Something is consequently inaugurated by the
Kantian repetition.[23]

Moreover, the said philosophical tradition *also* repeatedly roots
itself in this inauguration, at least if it is in fact true that a *philosophical* tradition as such becomes possible only from the point

where it, insofar as it takes as its object and condition its own presentation, produces the category and the problem of Darstellung. Because it is under the name of this category and in the face of this problem that something can from this point on present, exhibit, and designate itself as *philosophy*. It is not a question of proposing here who knows what inept break in the history of philosophy, but rather of showing that this history (which, moreover, belongs to the metaphysical treatise only from Kant onward, and from the last chapter of the first *Critique*) only takes place as history of *philosophy* under the Kantian condition. The *kant* of philosophy is what therein incessantly repeats itself in order to present itself, once only, under the signature of Kant; under this *kant*, and only under this cant, is the category and the problem of philosophy, *per genus proximum* (by *genre*—what is the genre of science?) *et differentiam specificam* (of philosophical, literary, popular, and scholarly species that differentiate themselves in philosophy) wholly defined.

(November 30, 1923, Louis Aragon begins a section in the *Paris Journal* called "The Starry Sky." The first article, devoted to Apollinaire, has as its epigraph the famous sentence by Kant, "Two things. . . . "[24])

At the same time, however, we can see that the exhibition of philosophy "as such" does not simply correspond to a restatement of the traditional ascetic imperative. Kant does not merely restate what Plato or Nietzsche restated already before him, and which the Antichrist will repeat in turn after him—namely, that "the service of truth is the hardest service."[25] And this, precisely because "form" is from now on the stake of philosophical "foundation" [*fond*], and of its resources [*fonds*]. This means, in effect, that critical *truth* cannot content itself with rigorously overseeing the conformity of its presentation with the external world. The text we cited above might allow one to think so. But only on the condition that one does not sublate the singular indeterminacy of the "truth" that Kant invokes therein, and that one just takes it as the classical correspondence between thought and the thing, which has as its external consequence the correspondence of thinking and its expression. In Kant's text, "truth" only intervenes under the guise of a warning against a certain "madness." Even so, truth as mental sanity is not the whole of critical truth, which needs to be considered on its own terms. (Or, rather, and which paradoxically comes out to be the *same* thing, a "transcendental sanity" constitutes the proper nature of critical truth and maintains it at a remove from classical truth. But we shall speak more about this health later on.)

Critical truth holds onto the traditional definition of truth—*adequatio rei et intellectus*—only as a formal or nominal definition. In its real definition, "transcendental truth" is the "objective reality" of concepts;[26] objective reality (*Realität*) is the condition of possibility for grasping something in its actuality (*Wirklichkeit*), that is to say, that it constitutes and commands the process of the presentation of the concept in intuition (by schematism). In other words, the value of *truth* resides in its character as the condition of presentation (in experience). One can always let it be said that *adequatio* probably implies a *praesentatio* necessarily. But the latter is thereby somehow included in the former: the adequation of the mind to a *res* implies in general the presence of this *res*. Whereas in Kantian presentation not all *res* are equal due to the restricted condition of possible experience, that is to say, due to the actual [*effective*] presencing in the reality [*effectivité*] open to the positive [*effective*] grasp of human reason. In transcendental truth, the exactitude of adequation becomes—if indeed this is a "becoming," though in any case it takes place by way of *kant*—the synthesis of presentation. It is not for synthesis to be adequate *to* a thing; it *makes* the adequation by which the thing presents itself. Truth thus does not have to oversee the conformity of an operation [*execution*]; rather, its task is to carry *itself* out [*s'executer*], or present *itself*—and, in particular, if one may say so, to *present itself as philosophy*.

Kant, sir. Another balloon lofted for the amusement of fools. —Balzac, *La Peau de chagrin*

The essence of truth is thus implicated as philosophy, and philosophy is implicated as (its) Darstellung. Which means that Darstellung *as such* (presenting [*mise en presence*], staging, genre, or style) insists on a specific demand leading all the way to the bitter asceticism of presentation [*l'exposé*]. We should not forget that here displeasure is a necessary mediation in view of pleasure—and that perhaps there is no Darstellung without pleasure. This is because elegance is desirable to the extent that, according to the terms of the preface, it happens that the greatest number "take pleasure" in the *Critique*.

In these conditions, it may turn out that science deprives itself of honey only with the intention of having far more exquisite jouissances. The note about children's play cups includes, just before the lines we have cited, the following:

> Without aesthetic assistance, distinct cognition contains a source of gratification solely through the charm of the object achieved through logical perfection, that is the correctness [*crossed out:* of exposition] and order in which it is considered, which exceeds all aesthetic perfection in both magnitude and duration. Archimedes' gratification in the bath. Kepler's at the discovery of a proposition. (*NF*, 529 [translation modified])

One could comment these lines at great length—and concerning "Kepler" in particular, who is not far from Copernicus, with whom the author of the second preface of the *Critique of Pure Reason* identifies. . . . So far as Kepler's pleasure, one can find it mentioned in the *Observations on the Feeling of the Beautiful and the Sublime* of 1764, where it is evident that it's a question of the very special seduction of "high intellectual insights" that remain at a distance from the "feeling of the beautiful and the sublime."[27] Kant simultaneously designates and dissimulates, as if with a wink, his pleasure, his theoretical pleasure, or the pleasure of a theoretician. But this ambiguous gesture is precisely what gives rise to the question: Which pleasure can be in question here? In a certain way, we have already been brought to naming it: the *impassive jouissance* of science. But what is this jouissance? Its impassivity seems to invoke its impossibility. And yet, taking Kant at his word, it exists and is certain—it is even, one might say, mathematically certain. What, therefore, is this pleasure? And how does one get ahold of it? What kind of necessity can there be in cognition, and out of what presentation can it arise?

But must we first give some credit to the note we have just cited, so old and so banal—to the point of verging on the frivolous, and at the very least the comical, with its reference to Archimedes' bath, the most hackneyed of the tradition, and which is more humorous than it is philosophical or scientific? If one poses this question, one must then also ask if Kant is still joking when, much later, in 1775 or in 1776, he notes (in terms of which some of the texts we have already cited permit us to suspect that they are not simply "pre-critical"):

> Philosophy: quid. Witz.
> Mathematics: Quotients [*quoties*]. Imagination.[28]

This can probably be translated as follows: the production of magnitudes as mathematical figures must be distinguished from the presentation of the thing in philosophy, which arises from a particular kind of mind: the sagacious, perceptive, analogical, and playful, the *esprit* of invention without rules and fiction.—However, such a translation is perhaps itself feigned or invented. For his part, Kant himself did not provide one. It is true at least that, like all translations, it is not without its problems. But Kantian philosophy skirted these problems just as carefully as it itself fabricated or invented them.

"Article 2.—All the essays published ought to have either a historical, philosophical, or aesthetic content, and in addition must be comprehensible to those unversed in the sciences." (An excerpt from a contract pertaining to the creation of the journal *The Hours* between Schiller and the publisher Cotta.

Schiller sent this contract to Kant together with a request for collaboration. One reads in Schiller's letter the following: "The journal will be read by an entirely other public than the one that has nourished itself on your writings, and the author of the *Critique* certainly also has things to say to it, and is the only one who would be able to do so successfully." June 13, 1794.—Kant, encouraged by Schiller and Fichte, responds only the following year, and then only to put off his participation to the distant future; *it was the day of Greek calends.*)[29]

§ 5   *Darstellung* and *Dichtung*

These unseasonable dozings exposed him
to another danger. He fell repeatedly, whilst
reading, with his head into the candles; a cot-
ton nightcap which he wore, was instantly in
a blaze, and flaming about his head. Whenever this happened, Kant behaved with great
presence of mind. Disregarding pain, he
seized the blazing cap, drew it from his head,
laid it quietly on the floor, and trod out the
flames with his feet. —Thomas De Quincey,
"The Last Days of Immanuel Kant"

What is needed, therefore, is an elegance of style that allows for
not even the slightest obscurity. In this lies the question of science
as such. This is because—as we have been able to read—science,
as such must not be beautiful; yet, as we have come to understand,
science, as such, has to darstellen [*present*] itself.[1] Darstellung is
prescribed at least twice in and for science: first, as the presentation of the object, the objecthood of which founds and guarantees
the objectivity of knowledge; the *phenomenality* of the object is
thus, in some way, both its presentability at the heart of a possible experience and its transcendental *exposition* as the condition
of possibility for experience. However, second, this exposition is
itself the discourse of the science of the phenomenon, which has

68

to present itself in accordance with the latter's conditions of presentation, and which requires, as we have seen, that this science
must present itself as *discourse*, in contrast to mathematics (which
does not present the *existence* of objects in experience).

These two requirements actually add up to only one, which
can be summed up in the following formula: *thinking the thing
as a presentation* (as a PHENO-menon) *implies the presentation of
thought*. For this reason, in one way or another, and whatever else
it might imply, thought doubtless entails a *beautiful* presentation,
or, more precisely, a presentation according to a certain *art*, if art
in general is the regime of sensible presentation [*mise en présence*]
or staging [*mise en scène*]. The establishment of mathematics as the
model for the presentation of the concept in intuition stamps this
model itself on philosophy; yet the exclusion of mathematics (or
a resection and redistribution of its beauty and the elegance of its
style) leaves the trouble of reproducing (both well and badly) this
same mathematical model up to a certain philosophical art.

Thus a beautiful presentation is needed—yet only in such a way
that it does not turn beauty into a predicate but rather into the
very substance of the presentation—into, to be more accurate, the
phenomenality "itself" of the phenomenon. This motif forms a
chain linking the beginning of the Analytic in the first *Critique*
to the third *Critique*: it is the chain through which the object is
produced in *harmony* and *as* harmony: "The imagination must
form an image (*Bild*) of the manifold provided by intuition"; as
image, figure, form, or formation—or even, if one so desires, as
tableau—the Bild assumes and manifests at once the "unity with
which all phenomena . . . ought to be already a priori in relation
and in harmony" (*CJ*, 26).[2] This harmony determines the aesthetic
and teleological investigations of the third *Critique* insofar as it
is a harmony *with* and *for* the needs of our understanding (that
is, its transcendental condition, since there can be no question of
presenting a harmony in itself): "In thinking of nature as harmo-
nizing . . . with our need to find universal principles . . . we must,
as far as our insight goes, judge this harmony as contingent, yet as
also indispensable for the needs of our understanding" (*CJ*, 26).

Nevertheless, it is this necessity itself that also makes beauty into a contingent predicate of presentation—or shatters the harmony of a presentation in the very moment it makes its request. This is because to think the thing as a phenomenal presentation implies *by this very fact* the thinking of the perceptible limitation of the thing (limitation, demarcation—*Absonderung*—without which *there would be no contour in general*, that is to say, neither a phenomenon in its reality, nor a form, surface, or outline for the *Critique*). Presentation is thus defined as the demarcation of presentation by thought (by contrast, the thought of adequation characterizes this presentation as coextension, which sheds no light on the question of possible limits). That is how this thought conceives itself philosophically as *exposition*. In other words, in a very specific way, it itself excludes the very thing that founds or structures it: a unity without remainder and the final harmony. Philosophy syncopates its own foundation: that is how it forms *itself*. The status of exposition as such is based on dismissing a certain beauty, but that is how (philosophical and critical) exposition turns its own beauty into a problem. Since, properly speaking, *beauty* (if it can ever be said *properly*) is thus probably that which appears—and, curiously, that which presents itself—in the very process of this internal exclusion or as its own product.[3] The beauty of exposition is thus the beautiful *nature* of presentation and, therefore, also the unattainable harmony of mathematics now become, through its relative exteriority, the supplementary quality that discourse *desires* (having, as it were, produced itself *outside itself*, and, in connection with this, one would have to investigate the frequent connection between feminine beauty and fainting in literature). From this simultaneously engender themselves, under the signature of Kant, an author and his other, an author-philosopher and his other, the former desiring the stylistic elegance of the latter.

∿

From this point on, one can see that this elegance of style, at once desirable and suspect, like the writer simultaneously engen-

dered and denied—or, to repeat what we've already said, this dis-
appointing presentation—is at the same time nothing other than
philosophy and the philosopher, and these *properly* speaking. Undecidable (wouldn't this be the very property of the proper), this
property combines the (de)monstrative authority of science *and*
the step-by-step discursive procedure of exposition. In fact, the
plea, the hope, or the desire of the preface to the first *Critique* aims
at bottom for the self-assurance that *at least one other* preface by
Kant feigns—one that is by coincidence the preface of a work on
ethics, the *Metaphysics of Morals*—when it declares the following:

> The Introduction that follows presents and to
> some degree makes intuitive the form which
> the system will take in both these parts [that
> is, the doctrine of right and the doctrine of
> virtue]. (*MM*, 365)

(Having just quoted Kant, Cournot writes,
"Doubtless a French reader has the right to be
shocked by the obscurity and crudity of this
technical language; however, it is not without
explanation, and when one comes to understand it, it presents a perfectly lucid sense."
—*Considerations . . .*)[4]

A fragile self-assurance, however, since presentation in intuition
is only ever "partial"—and we will never be done with questioning
this "part," if even one should speak here of questioning rather
than of perplexity; since, moreover, it is a question of *re*-presenta-
tion, of *Vorstellung* and not Darstellung (another perplexity because nowhere does Kant develop a rigorous concept of Vorstellung, the term for which covers, in places, the products of all the
faculties of the intellect), and since, finally, in the course of its
development, which we have already had an opportunity to read
(à propos of "Mr. Garve" and "logodaedalus"), this text will nevertheless plunge itself yet once more into problems of popularity.

One cannot, therefore, say that philosophy decides on its presentation cognizant of the cause and in full possession of its facul-

ties. One can only say that in this complex gesture, in this double postulation in which philosophy simultaneously embraces and demarcates itself, Darstellung presents itself as the trace (internal? internal/external?) of its own limits. Limited in principle (since art is "arrested" somewhere . . .), the beautiful is limiting. This is why the general problem of critical limits that guides the entire Kantian project has to be treated in relation to an essentially aesthetic problematic; that is, unless it is the other way around, and every aesthetic problematic is essentially one of limits, of delimitation as such, and of the plurality *of limits* that it engenders. Whatever may be the case, Darstellung separates itself from itself in itself, and it does so in two ways:

1. It defines itself (or substitutes itself for the definition) and renders itself finite [*se finitise*] in *exposition*;

2. At the same time, it enters into an ambivalent relation with something else called *Dichtung* that it pushes away and by means of which it perhaps also de-fines or in-finitizes [*dé-finit*] itself.[5]

It [philosophy] is poetry beyond the limits of experience . . . also essentially in images. Mathematical presentation is not a part of the essence of philosophy. The overcoming of knowledge by means of the power to *fashion myths. Kant* is remarkable—knowledge and faith! —Nietzsche, *The Philosopher's Book*[6]

⌒

Darstellung and Dichtung do not relate to each other as philosophy and literature. Not yet. It would be more appropriate to say that the second opposition (or apposition) becomes possible only once the first has produced its own effects within the Kantian problematization of exposition. It is precisely the proper of these effects to engender literary effects in philosophy and vice versa—effects that simultaneously distinguish and blur the efficacy and reality of one and the other.

Thus, one should not be in a hurry to translate *Dichtung* as "poetry"—even less so in Kant than elsewhere—although one ought not forget to hear the resonance of *Poetry*, which is very close [*Dichtkunst*], the art of *dichten*, for which in German—that is, in the modern Greek—one already then just as easily said *Poesy*. It would thus not be impertinent to begin from there and say that *Dichtung* is *dichten* without art, or not yet defined as art. *Dichten* is to put down in writing, to compose [*composer*]—far before such a notion is restricted only to literary composition. *Dichten is therefore darstellen* in the domain of written language. For philosophy, however, Dichtung names the delimitation through which it can sense itself in itself—or exclude itself. *Dichtung* is the mode of production that science can in no way acknowledge.

> All true metaphysics is drawn from the essence of the faculty of thinking itself, and is in no way fictitiously invented [*erdichtet*]. . . . [7]

A mule galloped down the mountain of science.—What is your name? asks Kant.—My name is Patience. . . . O Kant, the mule is a mule, and Kant is only a mind. —Victor Hugo, *The Ass*[8]

The impurity of its source or its pedigree is thus what defines Dichtung, and not some prior opposition between the true and the false, and even less one between the real and the imaginary. This is because the first of these oppositions will be thinkable only once a synthesis has been obtained from a *pure* source; imagination, for its part, will be the "blind but indispensable" producer of synthesis. Dichten or *erdichten*, "to poetize" [or, "to fiction"] is to tap a source other than that of pure reason; or, rather, it is to disturb or pollute this source. One suspects that this "definition," or position, will have difficulty working without problems if "pure" reason is not a normative point of reference preferable over other criteria (scientific, ethical, or aesthetic), but the originary instance *itself*, the *unique* source that Critique does not choose but is content to examine, and from which flows every possibility of scientific, ethical, or aesthetic decision, as well as every possibility

of presentation, either of the image or the concept, or of signification. *Pure* reason opens vertiginously onto the exclusivity of its
own foundation, where dichten and darstellung become indistin-
guishable.

In any case, it is only in that it derives from this first determination (as rigorously determined as it is undetermined by it: undecidable) that Dichtung is able to then give rise *after the fact* to the
opposition of science and of something that resembles the generic
image of literature. Therefore, in order to conceive *The Idea for a
Universal History with a Cosmopolitan Intent* (1784), Kant opposes
the idea of a "system" to that which could only be described as a
"novel."[9] In this case, the "system" is neither given nor constructed,
but in order to delimit its idea, in order to draw up its blueprint, a
negative is necessary, or, at the very least a background to set it off
against. The *novel* is the system, though an impure one.

Thus the genre that will come to be called "literature" demarcates itself from within philosophy. And the passage to literature
is itself in the first place a question of a certain genre or a certain
tone that one can adopt in philosophy. *Tone* is in general a property of all speech because "every linguistic expression has in its
context . . . a tone appropriate to its meaning. This tone indicates,
more or less, an affect of the speaker and in turn induces the same
affect in the listener, too" (*CJ*, 198). What is the tone of philosophy, the right philosophical tone? Kant defines it in 1796 in *On a
Newly Arisen Superior Tone in Philosophy*, where it is obviously by
standardizing its tone, that is to say, its functions, that philosophy
defines *its* literature, and the ethic of presentation imposes its "stylistic guidelines."[10]

It is a matter, therefore, of humbling the *superior tone* [grand-
seigneur] adopted by certain philosophers who affect genius, as
had already certain others in 1781 (one recalls that in his preface to
the first *Critique*, Kant evokes "the tone in vogue, whereby people
employ in their thinking a freedom that befits [only] a genius")
(*CPR*, 6).

To Kant:
You call superior the tone or the demeanor
of the prophets of our day. Let's be less ambiguous: for philosophy, the discourse of
the superior tone is really inferior thought.
—Friedrich Schiller

These are the philosophers of intuition and feeling, in short
those who believe in the possibility of the *presentation* of the supersensible, for example, of the moral law in the figure of the veiled
Isis. Here, exaltation and poetry go hand in hand—or rather exaltation, that which exceeds limits, defines *poetry* in the same way
that affect defines tone. And rather than looking to make a change
in tone, for Kant, these exalted philosophers need to be reduced
to silence.

This reduction occurs in two steps. Even as he grants that, in
fact, one "falls to one's knees" in front of the same "veiled goddess"
on both sides of the argument, and consequently, morality is res-
cued in both camps up to a certain point (it remains to be seen if
they are not in fact adoring the veil, while Kant prays to the goddess *herself*), the critical philosopher notes that in relation to the
"philosophical" process of practical reason, "the personified figure"
of "the veiled Isis" is an

> aesthetic mode of representing precisely the
> same object; one can doubtless use this mode
> of representation backward, after the first
> procedure has already purified the principles,
> in order to enliven those ideas by a sensible,
> albeit only analogical presentation, and yet
> one always runs the danger of falling into an
> exalting vision, which is the death of philoso-
> phy.[11]

In the place of Isis herself, we have already encountered the veil,
and we know that it is a Witz. In conformity with the ambiguity of the Witz, capable of "depth," the veil has performed twice,
once to lift itself and once to lower itself. For Kant, *for him* too,

the moral law—nondeducible and nonsensible—is a veiled goddess; nevertheless, the presentation of its effigy carries with it a mortal danger, even under the supervision of philosophy. The philosopher himself, the *pure* philosopher can grow uneasy—as if the danger resided less in the veiling as such, in the unveiling of the face of the law, than in the veil, in its *pleats* and its *movements*, which make him hesitate between concealing and revealing, as if he himself were undressed. The danger would lie, therefore, in the fact that the veil is itself the instrument of seduction (here, the seduction of the Law . . .), just as one recalls that the Witz spends a fortune in veils in order to conquer modesty without scaring it away. However, for the philosopher it is a matter of protecting himself against its seduction, which is threatening because it is also castrating: a little earlier in the text, in returning to the argument of one of his adversaries, Kant writes, " . . . and it is . . . in falsely attributed empirical properties (which are, for this exact reason, unfit for universal legislation) that reason is emasculated and crippled."[12] Isis Medusa.

Feelings standing in front of Kant's tomb:
Already the spirit of the unforgettable old
man, whose tomb we approach with tears
in our eyes, has fled its ashes and is looking
at the face of Truth, given without veil to
the sight of the blessed. —Poem by E. G. A.
Böckel, placed on the works of Kant during
his funeral.

It's better, therefore, to ban aesthetic presentation altogether. The presentation of science will be unadorned, even if it has to be a little crude.

I have known several systems of philosophy
and I have put considerable force into pen-
etrating them; but I can affirm that there
exists not a single one upon the face of the
earth, wherein the primitive matter of which
the Universe is composed may be characterized by traits as striking as in that of Kant. I

believe it impossible either to understand it better or to depict it better. He uses neither figures, nor symbols; he tells what he sees with a candor which would have been appalling to Pythagoras and Plato; for what the Koenigsberg professor advances concerning both the existence and the non-existence of this matter, and of its intuitive reality, and of its phenomenal illusion, and of its essential forms, time and space, and of the labor that the mind exercises upon this equivocal being, which, always being engendered, never, however, exists; all this, taught in the mysteries, was only clearly revealed to the initiate.
—Fabre d'Olivet, *The Golden Verses of Pythagoras*

The second step of the reduction is thus the following: Kant banishes the aesthetic in erecting the discourse of philosophy against all Isises, and in opposing the model invoked by philosophers who take the "superior tone," that is, the Plato whose exalted *Letters* he had condemned (and not without first floating a doubt about their authenticity) only a few pages earlier:

> For *Aristotle*, an extremely prosaic philosopher, certainly has the seal of antiquity about him, and according to the principle stated above, he has a claim to being read!—At bottom, all philosophy is indeed prosaic, and the suggestion that we should now start to philosophize poetically would be just as welcome as the suggestion that a businessman should in the future no longer write his account books in prose but rather in verse.[13]

In one and the same gesture, philosophy gives itself a trade and a style. Its trade is nothing other than accounting, though one shouldn't be in a hurry here to believe that Kant is humbling himself. First of all, we're in Königsberg, a city devoted to commerce, and in the home of the son of a merchant. Secondly, to keep the books of reason, the income and expenses of concepts, each appraised for its true value—is this not in effect the task of transcendental philosophy? *Critique* is a shop: its first preface said it well:

> For such a work of metaphysics is nothing but the *inventory*, put in systematic order, of all the possessions that we have through *pure reason*. (*CPR*, 13)

In regards to style, one can see that it is defined in and by philosophy: *Critique* brings about a manner of reading the tradition that guards a conception of a poetic classical philosophy, thereby [by contrast] establishing itself as a genre or a style—as if Plato, rather than having been condemned, were simply impossible to return to. Or, rather, thereby *barely* establishing itself as a style. This prose, itself compared to calculations, to columns of numbers—this prose somehow bound up with a mathematics that is itself debased and fallen into the empirical—constitutes a "style" apart from all style.[14] That which one might call philosophical *autology* excludes style:

> What method is for thought, style is for clear communication of thought to others. I have no need of style to do the same for myself.

says [*sic*] a note dating from between 1775 and 1780. So, if a note from the same period states that "we need words not only so that *others* may understand us, but so that we may understand *ourselves*," what we should grasp is that autology establishes thought as language, but it also establishes, conversely, if one may say it thus, its language as the zero degree of all language use, of all linguistic deviation and inflexion. Philosophy installs itself thus *not as merely another tone*—the tone of the shopkeeper as opposed to the tone of the superior [*grand-seigneur*], but as *the absence of tone*, the absence of the seductive, contagiously affect-laden voice, the absence of the veiled voice—and thus as an atonal exposition that can only be modeled on the book conceived as a well-armored treatise. Prose is the palliative of the mathematical shield. Prose permanently guards against death.

In the same year, 1796, in the *Announcement of the Near Conclusion of a Treaty for Eternal Peace in Philosophy*, Kant is also capable of going so far as reversing established values.[15] In response to a reproach made to critical philosophy for its "crude, *barbarous* language," he says:

> Whereas it is, on the contrary, an expression *de bel esprit* [sic] dragged into the philosophy of the elements of human knowledge that must be seen as barbaric.[16]

The term "bel esprit," in L. Guillermit's very close French translation of the expression *ein schöngeisterischer Ausdruck*, includes in the range of its meanings, "spirit" as such [that is, *esprit*, from the German *Geist*—Trans.], Witz (beauty as a dangerous predicate), but it also means, following Guillermit's formula, a "beautiful *literary* style." The latter translation is at least as justified as "mind," our own provisional version. It is, in fact, with the expression "schöngeisterischer Literatur," among others, that literature, in the original meaning of this term, would become in Germany what was called at that time in France "belles lettres."[17] Letters are only literary when they are beautiful. So, to repeat: literature is the product—or the remains—of a resection of the beautiful implemented according to a mathematico-metaphysical program.

This operation—truly singular, difficult to localize, and never clearly resolved [*décidée*] by philosophy—as we can see, has its immediate, efficient, and final causes in philosophy. Prose guarantees the discourse of every literature—it guarantees, in other words, the unadulterated purity of reason, by closing the eyes, the ears, and even the mouth of the thinker. The institution of *pure* reason—the very gesture of critique, that is, of ontology as the autolegislation of reason—requires the preservation of this purity, which, at the same time, requires the production of the *impure* mode of production, Dichtung, so that it may conjure and separate itself from this dangerous impurity (impure because it is beautiful? beautiful be-

cause it is impure?). It thereby names *literature* everything it held
at a distance from its autology, all the rest, all its remains.[18]

But the partition [*partage*] so achieved is not a simple one.

> Whoever wants to devote themselves to lit-
> erature, even if it were merely to belles lettres,
> should study the works of Kant, and do so
> not solely for their content, but also because
> of the logical rigor of their form. There is
> nothing better to accustom one to clarity, to
> fine distinctions, and to precision than this
> study. For the poet, these qualities possess a
> dazzling necessity. —Grillparzer, *Journal*

Produced on the outside of philosophy by the barbaric charms
of a veiled Medusa, Dichtung is also discovered—by the way, not
without chagrin, as we've already mentioned—in the exalted *Letters* of a certain Plato, that is to say, somewhere on the inside of
philosophy.[19] And this isn't the only the reason for which Dichtung is also produced, *at the same time, inside* philosophy. It is so
produced for a fundamental reason that stems from a vacillation
or a syncope in its groundwork. On the one hand, in effect, the
discourse of philosophy cannot not be produced through exci-
sion, incision, or the redelineation *of* (mathematico-metaphysical) Darstellung itself. Darstellung *itself undecides itself, inscribes
itself as an undecidable proposition, or inscribes the undecidability of
the philosophical proposition.* Discourse does not entirely have, in
principle, the purity that is in question here. On the other hand,
as soon as the philosophical suppression of *tone* announces itself
as prose (and how else would it announce itself, except perhaps as
a "silence" that would only be yet one more avatar of poetico-re-
ligious exaltation . . .), it cannot not announce itself at the same
time as being *already* a partition [*partage*] of literature itself. So
long as pure reason consumes itself in turning back toward its origin, it always already finds some Darstellung and always already
some literature. Discourse is not entirely the total absence of style
that ought to be in question here.

M. Jourdain: No, I want neither prose nor
poetry.
Grammarian: It has to be one or the other.[20]

~

Thus, philosophy imposes upon itself *a* style. Who knows even
if, in repudiating Dichtung and literature, the philosopher is not
rather looking, against Medusa-Isis, to preserve *the* style—the absolute style of elegant, solid exposition, pleasing and scientific,
popular and scholastic, this style that is always desired, and that
the desire of the philosopher would have simply deferred by means
of expert calculations, in order to better exhibit and enjoy it? The
elegance that Kant is so suspicious of is, we know, the elegance
that Kant the writer regrets being incapable of—or of not having
the time to devote his talent to (which is entirely different; perhaps
the muddle of Kant's excuses will begin to be illuminated by an
obscure glow). But it may also be the case that this rancor or this
disdain can only be considered in regard to a Dichtung inscribed
within philosophical discourse itself, in its prose. Although, it so
happens that Kant in fact inscribes it by means of a gesture that simultaneously doubles and undoes the scientific gesture. Kant *also*
presents himself as a poet-philosopher. The preface to the *Critique
of Practical Reason* allows us to read the detours, or the roundabout
manner that can be no more "indirect," by which this Darstellung
produces itself. It is a strange moment.

In the name of the "popularity" of moral knowledge, Kant de-
fends himself against "the reproach that I want to introduce a *new
language*" into philosophy (*CprR*, 145). He thus always responds to
the same reproach, which targets the "barbarous" manner, bristling
with scholastic technicality, coarse and obscure, of his style. He
takes this defense as a pretext to justify—once again, and without
deploring any absence of elegance—the language of the first *Critique*. In an ironic challenge—as he relates the outcome of his "expression" to that of his thoughts themselves, the solidity of which,
we know, is imperturbable—he proposes to the reader that he or

she furnish him with "more popular expressions that are still just as suitable to the thought" (*CprR*, 145). The autological autarchy of the language of philosophy is thus proclaimed to be without appeal. A long note is added to this proclamation in which Kant declares that he fears the obscurities of his language more than the confusions that everyday language gives rise to (and which doesn't distinguish, or does so badly, between the oppositions permitted/forbidden and in conformity with/contrary to duty). He is concerned, therefore, as is the case in another text we have already read, about the precision that multiplies notions and terms. However, it turns out here, as it does in the other text (which figures further on in the same *Critique*), that the fine distinctions required by philosophy are not necessarily "foreign to ordinary language." Which turns out to be the case, in fact, exactly in the example that he gives; if one observes ordinary language more closely, one shall see that the polarity permitted/forbidden is related to a "practical rule that is simply possible," whereas duty concerns a necessary legality of reason. One can show by way of example the presence of concepts in language. For example:

> Thus, for example, it is *forbidden* to an orator, as such, to forge new words or constructions; this is to some extent permitted to a poet; in neither case is there any thought of duty. (*CprR*, 145)

It is probably not irrelevant that this entire discussion is recapitulated and illustrated by an example that pertains to the fundamental concept of Kant's entire ethics, that of pure duty. Since, from this perspective, the example at least allows it to be stated that the poet, in his innovative, irregular, indeed transgressive activity remains morally irreproachable (by the same token, one recalls that, to a certain extent, the morality itself of the superiors [*grand-seigneurs*] was less suspect than their statue of Isis as such). But on the face of it—or *almost* on the face of it—this example contains more than this morality. Or rather, its exemplarity is relevant in the first place for the morality of language and in language:

language knows how to articulate the difference between certain concepts. But it turns out later that it knows it in a way that is exemplary for the one who innovates and who fabricates in language itself. We already know this figure: he is called Logodaedalus. But here it turns out that in sum there are two Logodaedaluses. The first is the same as the previous one: the charlatan orator; the second is the poet. Yet, the poet is exemplary here in that he does the same thing as Kant: he introduces a new language. Such is the detour, almost vertiginous, by which this note ties itself to the initial motif of the text. These lines serve, in sum, to identify—in small, tightly spaced letters on the bottom of the page and as if off the page—the model of the one who may allow himself to innovate in language. It's the poet, and according to *his example*, the philosopher finds himself justified, morally justified, in his barbarous innovations. This note is written (by whom and by what? That is another story. . . . —By kant perhaps . . .) in order to simultaneously publicize and censor the following proclamation: *I, Immanuel Kant, am as a philosopher a Poet.* I am, as a philosopher, a poet, and I therein violate nothing of the philosophical ethic of presentation. Which means two things:

1. That the philosopher is a Dichter, a composer, which is to say that he "forges" (the word is found in the text on "new language"), composes, produces, or invents new words, according to the most serious and imperious necessity of thought; as it is not a question of fabricating by way of a "puerile" artifice and in order to distinguish oneself, it is not a matter, still according to the same text, "of the '*künsteln*' of new words," or of being mannered or acting the artist.

2. But that the example—and the moral example as much as the aesthetic one—of this philosophical Dichtung is found in the poet, in the Dichter of belles lettres; in other words, the philosopher must play the artist—however one wishes to understand this, since, in the end, if *künsteln* is ridiculous when it is only ceremonial, by contrast thought can demand here and there a *Künstlerei* of philosophy—a logodaedalie.

～

Kant's surreptitious procedure carefully veils the identification of the poet and the philosopher—as much as it results in an exhibition that can hardly be described as modest. Here again, exorbitant quantities of ingenuity have been spent in order to throw a veil over something or someone—someone whose image is at once rendered seductive.

This seduction does not address [*tient à*] only the vanity of the philosopher. Or, to be more precise, it is not simply interested in it [*n'y tient pas*], because this vanity is inextricably mixed up with the most innate and imperious philosophical desire for exposition. Defending the language of philosophy consists in defending a Dichtung that, in itself, has nothing to do with poetry—but which arises out of Darstellung itself. Darstellung requires a Dichtung because, as *exposition*, it has already deprived itself of a direct and pure Darstellung. It's therefore exposition that requires, for its Darstellung or *in the guise* of a Darstellung, a Dichtung. The latter must be a palliative, the mantle of a presentation stripped naked and mutilated. But philosophical Dichtung does not exist exactly in this way: in principle, there can be no *properly* philosophical Dichtung. The reason for this: *neither is there any* philosophy *delimited as such so long as the "system" which desires that the impossibility of Darstellung engender its supplemention with the impropriety of Dichtung has not been put into place.* More precisely still: *the impropriety of Dichtung is not a quality that inheres in an entity called "Dichtung"* (it is specifically not a property), which would hold itself in front of and outside of Darstellung; rather, *the improper regime called "Dichtung" is engendered in the syncope of Darstellung.*

Such is, therefore, the lot of dichten—of making, of know-how, and of the know-how of composition—that it can only properly present itself in the improper model of poetry.—Presentation skirted, diverted, a production itself erdichtet [poetized—Trans.], feigned or trafficked, logodaedalic, of the poet-philosopher—who perhaps realizes [*rendre compte*] (insofar as one can here, like a shopkeeper, account for [*tenir compte*]) the incoherency of the

declarations of Kant-the-writer. When the latter regrets his lack
of talent, this ought to be understood as the inability to guarantee
a veritable philosophical poetry, and in moments when he regrets
his lack of time or youth, this ought to be taken to imply a disdain
for the dangerous futility of the task of giving literary form to
something. A double hypocrisy, consequently, the motifs of which,
moreover, can be crossed.

∼

But this double hypocrisy is perhaps at the same time a double
sincerity. Since, in fact, philosophical Dichtung does not arrive,
in spite of everything, "in person," to the extent that the *system*
itself—Darstellung—is *always* expected.[21] The desire for elegance
actually desires something the taking place of which remains problematic. By the same token, the image of the poet is thus the only
possible model *and*, at the same time, the only possible foil—and
this simply because the poet is a philosophical character. The question of Darstellung is the question of Dichtung, of the autonomous composition of a discourse confronted by its own alterity
and its own deterioration. Consequently, as suspect, puerile, and
attention-seeking as a poet can be—as exalted and imprudently
adoring an admirer of Medusa as he may be, as the Dichter, he
is a depository, analogically at least (and there is no other), of the
ideal of discourse, of Darstellung. Dichtung is probably a lack of
Darstellung; however, it is also the *type* for a production based on
the purity of an autonomous source.[22] The poet-philosopher "is"
the mathematician who would write (in prose). Which amounts to
saying that he *is* nothing, or that he is a monstrous, untenable hy-
brid. That is nonetheless how he forms the *type* for exposition. He
is the one who knows how to compose a presentation out of himself. The poet is an *author*: it is of him that one says: "Now there's
a *Euclid*," "there's a Kant," "there's a Wieland." The authority of
the author combines the purity of the source and the *ingenium* (le
Witz) of inspiration.

However, as a result, this combination is untenable: the poet

is irremediably split [*partage*] between autological autonomy and
its obscure or lethal face, exaltation, vulgarity, or the face of Isis.
It is impossible to grasp one without at least touching the other,
because *it's the same*. The same undecides itself. Contamination—
perhaps a certain madness—is inevitable in one sense just as much
as in the other. Literature is in philosophy: not because it entered
into it, as we have seen, but because it "came out" of it. Philosophy should be good literature. But in principle, literature is inevitably . . . all the rest, that is, always bad literature. . . .

> Why is a mediocre poem intolerable, but a
> mediocre speech still quite bearable? The rea-
> son appears to lie in the fact that the solem-
> nity of tone in every poetic product arouses
> great expectations and, precisely because
> these expectations are not satisfied, the poem
> usually sinks even lower than its prose value
> would perhaps merit. (*A*, 146)

(but what takes place when a work in prose makes one await . . . its
own poetry?)

> The philosopher of Königsberg . . . is the
> most poetic of philosophers and worthy of his
> great posterity, wherein, in German philoso-
> phy, we have seen come together the great-
> ness of sentiment and the rigors of thought.
> —Alain, *Letters to Serbio Solmi on the Philoso-
> phy of Kant*

~

Therefore, the danger cannot be entirely warded off. This is
how elegance or literary pleasures are proscribed in philosophy.
Whatever may be the severity or coldness of science, she is not
able to entirely possess a certain aesthetic pleasure, for the lack of
which it will never be offered to a single spectator. It is *theory* as
such—that is to say, the *vision* of knowledge—that must be pre-

sented: "The unity of cognition" that reason requires "possesses a particular charm," and the critical procedure of this same knowledge, namely "the unity of cognition, when one takes care that the boundaries of the sciences do not run together, but rather each takes in its own separated field," "has also a special charm."[23] The theoretician tastes a pleasure that is sui generis, of a genre proper, indefinable perhaps, but which definitely communicates with the genre of literature:

> Beautiful cognition. Presentation of concepts.
> Beautiful language, eloquence and poetry.
> —A note by Kant[24]

That is why Kant, writer-philosopher, writer because philosopher, is himself the logodaedalus, the maker of words he stigmatizes. He is able to be so in at least two ways: either in opposition to charlatans of all kinds and varieties, he is the good logodaedalus, the one who draws and who composes even his words from the elements themselves of purity; however, nowhere does Kantianism offer a theory of language, of the purity, or of the originality of language; or, Kant himself can be nothing other than a *logodaedalus*, a maker of pompous or brilliant words, a maker of Witzes and veils. More probably—if there is any sense in speaking in this way—it is neither the one nor the other but the both of them at the *same* time, and this "same" Logodaedalus is first of all the one who makes or remakes the word "logodaedalus," thus repeating in his scholastic Latin, as if by chance, the rumor that mistakes Plato for a Byzantine rhetorician.[25] Kant thus replays the undecidable conflict, or the undecidable competition, between Plato and the sophists. He is thus on the side of the philosopher, of Plato: but in this repetition, Plato is already on the side of "logodaedalus". . . . Reinventing this word—"logodaedalus"—and signing his text with this Witz, Kant partitions [*partage*] and combines literature and philosophy in one stroke, each being for the other the most intimate menace and most powerful charm.

> A ridiculous and touching memory: the salon where one made one's first appearance

at eighteen, alone and without patronage! A woman's glance was enough to intimidate me. The harder I tried to please, the more awkward I became. I got quite the wrong ideas about everything; either I was confiding with no justification; or I saw a man as an enemy because he had looked at me gravely. But at that time, in the midst of the terrible misfortunes caused by my shyness, how really fine a fine day it was! —KANT (Stendhal, *The Red and the Black*, epigraph of part II, chapter 2.[26] An "apparently fanciful attribution," points out P. G. Castex, in his critical edition. Stendhal did not like Kant, as Castex also notes in citing a passage in *Rome, Naples, Florence* to which one can add the following: "Kant, Fichte, etc. superior men who did nothing but build erudite [*savants*] houses of cards." However, if one consults Stendhal's journals, for example on June 5, 1811, one will become quickly convinced that, in fact, the writer has with the name of the philosopher signed memories of himself.)

If by *literature* one understands what the term only started to mean in an exclusive or exhaustive way after 1790, namely, the category of the written production of *fictions* (Dichtungen), the nature of which requires this "inimitable" divergence called *style*—the divergence for Kant, we should recall, from Hume—a category that distinguishes (and/or combines) in itself its own *genres* (and, in the first instance, a prose and a poetry), and which engenders the concept of the "writer" as *author* (one who possesses their *own* style)—then Kantian discourse is the instrument and locus for the delimitation of this category. In other words, it is also the locus of its birth—or its *presentation*—and native soil. This particular literature is a property of philosophy—thus, perhaps it is not so surprising that Immanuel Kant has known such a singular fortune as a literary figure.

The desire for form took over them, they repudiated the desire for content, but the desire for play gathered them into a discussion so noisy and uninterrupted that they might have entirely forgotten the empirical as a whole, up to the last man if it weren't for Father Benno reminding them of it. Chewing all the while, the critic took pleasure in talking to them about his formal taste and in informing them that "he wanted to establish the limits of the original genres of poetry in their eternity" without taking into account empirical poets, who always begin a posteriori and whose imagination always shakes the limits of intelligible poetry (*Poesis noumenon*) given to understanding by prudent critical philosophy. —F. Nikolai, *Life and Opinions of Sempronius Gundiberts, German Philosopher*, a novel, 1798

It is by excluding *and* appropriating this literature, in securing its *lack* and monopolizing its dispossession that philosophy assures its autonomy *in spite of* the insufficiency of its armor (or its popularity). It establishes command and jurisdiction over its exposition across the entire domain of "composition." However, with the same gesture, philosophy also infects itself with what it has evacuated; thus, philosophy right away begins the trial (which must also be understood in its juridical sense, according to the tremendous figurative power of [Kant's] tribunal of reason) of a certain expropriation. Kant simultaneously implements a triple operation: he delimits the instances of Darstellung and Dichtung; he *arrests* each at a certain style, the former to a certain prose that ought to be the simple, graceless beauty of philosophical literature, but also, in the same gesture, he crosses these instances one with the other, and by this contamination, in *spite of everything*, or because the philosopher-writer has no model other than that of the Dichter, he sets into motion the expropriation or the displacement of the very system in which the *regulated* distinction, opposition, and sometimes even the combination of Darstellung and Dichtung is possible. This "system" does not hold [*ne tient pas*]. There is necessarily contamination, and thus an *unregulated* combination. Paradoxically, it is perhaps also after Kant that there can no longer be neither philosophy nor literature (we shall have to confirm this shortly). There will only be a permanent interference between these categories that will permanently seek to be written.

I have often had the thought that it should not be impossible to make the writings of the famous Kant, who complains so often about the imperfection of his Darstellung, comprehensible without taking anything away from their richness or robbing him of the Witz and originality evident in his excerpts. If it were permitted to give his works, with the understanding of course, that this correspond to his own Ideas—a better order, especially when it comes to the constructions of his periods and as it pertains to his episodes and repetitions. They should be able to become as comprehensible as the writings of Lessing. One doesn't need to allow oneself greater liberties than the ones the old critics took with classical poets, and I think that one would then see that Kant, considered from a purely literary point of view, belongs among the classical writers of our nation. —Friedrich Schlegel, *On Philosophy*

§ 6 The Sublime System and the Sick Genius

> The urge to compose verse that your high-ness exhibited during your illness reminds me of Socrates, who Plato says had a similar de-sire while he was in prison. I believe that this mood for versifying arises from a powerful agitation of the animal spirits that is capable of completely unsettling the imagination of those who do not have their minds firmly planted, and which heats women up a little bit more and disposes them to writing poetry. And I take this inclination as the mark of a mind that is more powerful and elevated than the average. —Descartes to Elizabeth, Febru-ary 22, 1649

(Kant in the feminine: *die Kante*, is the pointed, the thin and sharp edge, the angle, of a ridge or a divide.)

In a certain way, this very singular logodaedalie will have been Kant's "philosophy itself." Or, at the very least, the extreme limit—a complicated and intricate line—on which this philosophy would have tried to write itself. Which means that the complex gesture we have been pointing out up to now is indissociable from this philosophy's ultimate ambitions (arising from an ultimate necessity) to being a *system*. Aiming at the *system* presupposes, implies, and restricts all the motives of Darstellung, even its "essence." This implication is mutual: Darstellung demands and entails the system. The second "book" of this work, *Kosmotheoros*, will examine toward what and into what the system is thus driven.[1] But one must first repeat and recast the question of Logodaedalus inside the system as such.

Toward this end, we must penetrate further still into the Kantian logic of Dichtung. I do not use this expression by chance or by way of approximation. Dichtung brings with it its own proper *logic*, which is woven into or rather scattered throughout the transcendental logic. Which doesn't mean simply that one buttresses and controls the other. On the contrary, in the very least they repel each other as much as they attract each other, and their impact straightaway provokes—a priori—a certain displacement of the Kantian edifice. Their logic is that of a syncope, or of multiple crises of the syncope. And it is precisely this logic that makes Kantian "doctrine" the most abstruse, labyrinthine—and most "badly" written—philosophy. Syncopating its own discourse, it provokes the displacement of a "thinker" between a philosopher and a writer, and the displacement of a "writing" that suffers the torture of both being and not being one. One can probably thereby see, if one has not yet done so, that the question of writing has not been laboriously implanted in Kant by a modernity suffering from textual narcissism. The question of writing (which is, as we have seen, also the modern "question," despite appearances, of *tone*, as well as the question of *popularity*), reads in Kant like *an open book*. The book is so open, in fact, that the question arises whether philosophy will ever be able to close it again: and what gives itself to be read—painfully—is, in the final analysis, a sort of inscriptive displacement of ontology. This is not to say that the question of writing arrives from somewhere outside of ontology; rather, on the contrary it is the name of a network of breaks, fractures, or the *kant* with which ontology syncopates itself.

However, the logic of Dichtung also corresponds to a confusion—as we have started to see—between literature and philosophy. The values of rupture should not here be preferred to the values of combination: their coupling (*and not* their dialectic) constitutes, rather, the repetition, the exposition, or the dramatization of the "systemic" coupling, in the kant, of the discourse of *critique* and the discourse of *synthesis*. A naïve reading of what we have just written could make one believe that before kant there existed a syncretic unity of literature and philosophy, of heterology and autology. But the logic of Dichtung/Darstellung (. . . if one wrote in German, just as Kant, after all, allowed himself to do *in philosophy*, repeating the *popular* gesture of Descartes, one would have greater latitude to play at being Logodaedalus, and to speak the logic of *Dardichtung*. But in the first place, "one" (?) is not Kant; second, if "one" wrote in German, *the* language of philosophy, one would probably reproduce another Kant, the one who wrote his *Dissertatio* in *Latin*, for example. "One" would point out to us, because "one" recalled it above, that Kant was suspicious of elegance even in Latin; probably . . .)—the logic, therefore, of Dardichtung *also* corresponds to the confusion and obfuscation of a tradition established long before Kant. Not entirely that of the partition [*partage*] between philosophy and literature (since the modern concept of literature contains disarticulation itself; simultaneously, it implies an attempt to ignore, overcome, or fix this disarticulation). Rather, the partition [*partage*] of philosophy and poetry—such as Descartes was able to recognize it: a peaceful imparting [*partage*] of functions all devoted to the same truth, or such as Leibniz puts to work when, throughout the *New Essays on Human Understanding*, where he strives to place the resources of rhetoric and poetry (back) into the service of truth (and where he is doubtless debating more with Locke than on the point of innateness, and in which the more rationalist of the two is not whom we think).[2] In order to articulate the Kantian problematic of presentation, it is necessary to have effaced and obscured such a partition [*partage*], that is, the allocation [*partage*] that allows one to meticulously distinguish and unite, in the presentation of Truth, the *rigor* and the *glory* of this same Truth. The Kantian partition [*partage*] functions differently: although it distributes the roles (of tones, of writings), it is nonetheless also that it produces itself only in the collapse of a certain redistribution [*répartition*] of roles. Henceforth, the *philosopher* and the *writer* are not concerned with the same truth, which does not mean, however, that each has his own. Rather, it means that each is haunted by that of the other (of the same). Kant the writer is the anxious—obsessed, and as if distraught—figure who arises out of chaos, if indeed he doesn't in fact produce it.[3]

In all these ways, Critique—the work, the works, the "system," and their "author"—inscribes with a heavy hand, in between styles, unhappily, the broken logic of a violent disorder.

> . . . the wicked serpent in our bosom of the common language of the people gives us the best metaphor for the hypostatic union of the natures of the senses and of understanding, the idiomatic communication of their powers, the synthetic mystery of the two correspond-ing and self-contradictory forms a priori and a posteriori, the transubstantiation of subjec-tive conditions and subsumptions into objec-tive predicates and attributes by the copula of a command or expletive to attenuate the boredom, and to fill up the empty space in the periodic galimatias *per Thesin and An-tithesin.* —J. G. Hamann, *Metacritique of the Purism of Reason*[4]

So it goes, in particular, when it is a matter of Dichtung's trac-ing: at the same time as a crooked, almost shameful operation transfers the privilege of poetry to the account of philosophy, without, however, being able to suppress the mortal danger that hides therein (and which it veils)—at the same time, therefore, as this hard to determine and nearly illegible operation, another one carries over elsewhere, and on different terms, the ensemble of motifs and instances named "Dichtung." This "elsewhere" is not situated just anywhere. Above all, it is not, as one might still be led to mistakenly think, in a "particular charm" *added* to the system from the outside. If philosophy is literature, it is not so "by addition." The procedure of "aggregation," we know, is never suitable to the system as such; that place is reserved only for assimilation, which Kant scholastically calls "intussusception" (*per intus susceptionem*).[5] The aggregate, precisely, is chaos, the chaotic "aggregate" without the least trace of the "system,"[6] over and against which reason must conquer its own system in the name of the analogical rule of unity and finality. However, this rule (about the nature of which we do not, for the moment, have to pause) is the product, as we shall see, of Dichtung. Dichtung, both designated and effaced in the positing of the philosophical author, glimpsed beneath the philosopher's coat, is returned thus not to the surface or to the ornamentation of the system, but to its heart, or—to what is perhaps a better metaphor—to its nerve.

~

In effect, a double displacement is sufficient for Dichtung, apparently purloined from or forbidden to Critique, to reappear in this position: namely, by way of the "anthropology," and its consignment to sensibility. But, as we shall show, this double displacement—another evasion, another displacement—leads us right back to Critique's system.[7] Unless it is the system itself that constitutes itself, in critical philosophy, by means of displacements, transgressions, evasions, and unforeseen returns. . . .

In the *Anthropology*, the analysis of the imagination is continued with the analysis of the sensible *Dichtungsvermögen*, the sensible "power of invention" or "composition" (*A*, 67–68). This analysis, along with the entire analysis of the imagination, moves with difficulty between two requirements: first, the recognition of the *positive* power of imagination (of the empirical imagination that one must not confuse with transcendental imagination, but which in the *Critique of Pure Reason* nonetheless constitutes *the only model and point of reference* for "transcendental imagination"); second, the warning against the overwhelming series of dangers it comes with (the phantom, the grotesque, disgust, perversion, in short the *pathological* in general—to which the text does not cease to return with a troubling predilection . . .). In between these, and participating in both not without some hesitations, one finds the artist, the poet, the novelist. Yet also the transcendental philosopher.

Dichtung's capacity for sensibility subdivides, in effect, into three degrees: first, there is the Dichtung of form and formation (*Bildung*) in general; second, there is the Dichtung of association; third, that of affinity, which is perhaps the superior and most fully elaborated product of Dichtung: "The basis [*Grund*] for the possibility of the manifold's association, insofar as this basis lies in the object, is called the manifold's *affinity*" (*CPR*, 162). Radical and foundational, *affinity* was in the first *Critique* the name of the relation necessary to the phenomenal production of objects. Here, its definition is followed by some examples taken from the flow of conversation, or of reverie. This is because, far from being mechanical like association, affinity demands an activity of the understanding accompanied by the "play of the imagination, which nevertheless follows the laws of sensibility" (*A*, 70). The composition of affinities also implies an affinity—singular and remarkable—of the understanding and sensibility. It implies, therefore, taken in its broadest sense, the *synthesis* of which the whole of the theory of reason must draw the conditions of possibility.

As if it were necessary to return to the definition of the thing, Kant deems it necessary to indicate that *affinitas* is an analogy borrowed from chemistry (already, the first *Critique* spoke of a chemistry of pure reason—we shall return to it elsewhere). In chemistry, an "intellectual combination is analogous to an interaction of two specifically different physical substances intimately acting on each other and striving for unity, where this *union* brings about a third element that has properties that can only be produced by the union of two heterogeneous elements" (*A*, 70). And the analogy makes itself explicit thus:

> Despite their dissimilarity, understanding and sensibility by themselves form a close union for bringing about our cognition, as if one had its origin in the other, or both originated

> from a common origin; but this cannot be,
> or at least we cannot conceive how dissimilar
> things could sprout forth from the same root.
> (*A*, 70)

—To which a long note adds a general consideration on the enigma constituted by the union of unlikes in nature, and especially the union of the two sexes (to which the next paragraph will turn; we, too, shall return to it later). The chemistry of the "fraternal bond" was already a union of the sexes (in German as in French, "understanding" and "sensibility" are of opposite genders). The union of the sexes sanctions, so to speak, the status of affinitas, and through this, that of Dichtung in general: this union, writes Kant, is the chasm in front of which and into which reason loses itself. At the same time, it is the enigma that reason must confront in the name of synthesis. Or, more precisely, no doubt, the enigma of the union of the sexes is the last veil covering an even more formidable enigma: the enigma of the same, of the *same* source (that reason declared lost ever since the introduction to the first *Critique*).

This veil protects—because the mystery of the sexes is at least natural, and it is evident that it works, even if one doesn't exactly know how—but it is already itself dangerously translucent, or full of holes (and this, in particular, because of the *incest* of this "fraternal" union), or it moves: it opens itself, partway, onto the syncope of affinitas, or, worse still, on affinitas *as* the syncope of reason. This is moreover why, as we shall see in a moment, critical philosophy will attempt to contain this enigma by invoking the Immaculate Conception as its own most proper, or perhaps improper, Dichtung.

One can see what is at stake in this *poetic* (?) union of unlikes; it is enough to recall it summarily: nothing less than schematism, the nerve of transcendental logic, here presented or figured in a new version. The union of the category and of intuition, this "concealed art" of Critique, the condition of possibility of Darstellung in experience, constitutes here the superior power of Dichtung. And if it is still inconceivable or ungraspable (*unbegreiflich*) in the "Analytic of Principles," at least it gives itself in an image, in a chemical and sexual analogy, at least it is thus *gedichtet*. In Dichtung's capacity for sensibility, or *in the sensible figuration* of this power, that is, in the sensible figuration of the *power of sensible exposition*, is at work what makes the system possible in its functioning and in its very systematicity, since the Architectonic of the *Critique*, whether it be the "art of systems," needs precisely a *schema* in order to present the system, a schema of an "organism" that rests on the "affinity of parts." And this schema of the system constitutes (or *must* constitute) the ultimate jurisdiction of reason to the extent that it has to expound the cause of its own science.

One morning K. felt much fresher and more resilient than usual. Thoughts of the Court hardly intruded at all; or when they did, it seemed as if it would be easy enough to get a purchase on this immeasurably vast organism by means of some hidden lever which admittedly he would first have to grope for in the dark; but that then it would be child's play to grasp it, uproot the whole thing, and shatter it. —Franz Kafka, *The Trial*

But for the moment, this operation interests us for a more narrow reason: here, in the *Anthropology*, it couples the understanding and sensible imagination. However, if the power of Dichtung rests, according to the letter of the text, limited to sensibility, it thereby does not any less *touch* understanding with its point. And one will not be surprised to find this analysis of Dichtung repeated further on in regards to the *superior* powers of knowledge. The functions of Dichtung are thus replayed in the *talents*, in *Witz*, in *sagacity* and *genius*—which are constitutive of reason itself. The Dichtung of affinitas thus also forms an affinity of reason and (sensible) imagination.[8]

On the subject of genius, certainly, we will no longer speak of this Dichtung, and, at least for the most wary acceptations, so to speak, of "genius," we shall take the example of the Dichter-poet, who is right away surrounded by critical scrutiny, moral reservations, or psychopathological diagnoses. We shall have to return shortly to the "genius"; for the moment, let us recall what a double figure the poet cuts in Kant, and let us recall also that the genius always takes the stage, here and elsewhere, with the *philosophical* motifs of "invention" and "harmony" in creation—even if he were buffered with cautionary remarks (the passage we cited earlier on the scrutiny of "truth" in the "presentation of the object" is in the same §57 of the *Anthropology* about genius; this scrutiny is watching for the "madness" that is a possible excess of genius). These precautions thus do not prevent that, once again, and this time by way of a singular relation to the cornerstone of the system (the synthetic power of reason), a scene, or in the very least a production, rehearses and reconstitutes itself and comes apart all at once, that is to say, it disperses and displaces itself into terms that are heterogeneous, in *one* enigmatic figure; in this scene, the Dichter, when he falls, unveils the place of a *Darsteller* who faints in turn in his own impossibility and is obligated to pass the role off to, if not another Dichter, then at least to a *Schriftsteller*, a writer. The displacement reveals a pen that is perhaps mutilated. Just as Kant has already told us: when one lacks Hogarth's burin, then one has to describe, to write.

And one has to do so because of the system. Because the system, in its "cosmic concept" (different from its "scholastic concept": Are the cosmic and elegance thus somehow related?), of which the Architectonic demands the schema or the *monogram* and indicates the *type* "personified in the ideal of the philosopher," can be nothing less than the *sublime*: the sublime corresponds in effect to "a pretension" of "our reason [which] demands absolute totality as a real idea . . . " (*CJ*, 106).

However, one must learn that the sublime *is written*. Although at the same time (or with the same gesture), it itself occupies the thin and perilous line of partition [*partage*] that Dichtung traces, the line that cuts and disarticulates, *die Kante* of philosophy. One must also approach the sublime with circumspection, to say nothing of "romances and maudlin plays, insipid moral precepts" that are not sublime, one has to beware of all "excitations of the imagination" or of "the agreeable lassitude we feel after being stirred up by the play of affects" and which correspond to the massages prized by "Oriental voluptuaries . . . " (*CJ*, 133–34).

> At dawn, the household of Emmanuel Kant in Königsberg begins to stir. The flesh still warm from sleep, Maia and Al-Sufi, the two daughters of Kant's governess, stretch out voluptuously. (Exposition of the first scene in *The Young Man*, a play by J. Audureau, staged in 1973 by the Théâtre des Amandiers at Nanterre)

. . . however, one must consider in addition that enthusiasm, or the "idea of the good accompanied with emotion" is not the end all or be all of the sublime. Since

> (strange though it seems) even [the state of] *being without affects* (*apatheia, phlegma in significatu bono*) in a mind that vigorously pursues its immutable principles is sublime, and sublime in a far superior way, because it also has pure reason's liking on its side. Only a cast of mind of that sort is called noble— [though] the term has since come to be applied to things as well, such as a building, a garment, a literary style, a person's bearing, and so on—namely if it arouses not so much *amazement* [Verwunderung] (an affect [that occurs] when we present novelty that exceeds our expectation) as *admiration* [Bewunderung] (an amazement that does not cease once the novelty is gone), which happens when ideas in their exhibition harmonize, unintentionally and without art, without our aesthetic liking. (*CJ*, 132–33)

The only true nobility of the sublime is therefore apathy, the ab-

sence of affect and *tone*, that is to say, in effect, as we already knew,
an *edifice*: the architectonic of the system, an *article of clothing*: the
palliative [pallium] of presentation, a *manner of writing*: prose, a
posture, the deferent yet vigilant way of holding oneself in front
of the statue of Isis. But it's still a question of presentation, and
therefore of prose, a style without style, or of philosophy; more
precisely, of critical prose, this new language and this logodaedalie
permitted in spite of everything, this exposition graceful enough
that it must be admired, in spite of everything. Prose is sublime,
or

> *simplicity* (artless purposiveness) is, as it were,
> nature's style in the sublime. Hence it is
> also the style of morality, which is a second
> (namely, a supersensible) nature. (*CJ*, 136)

All the regrets, all the worries of Kant the writer—to the extent
that it was necessary to take these literally—probably find themselves here discretely effaced by the author of the Analytic of the
Sublime. Now there's a Kant, now there's the sublime. There is
certainly a sublime logodaedalie here, entirely prosaic, which im-
prints the presentation of morality, of moral *autonomy*, on a writing. Result: the presentation of the *end* of the system. The ethic of
presentation lies in the exposition of ethics.

(According to university traditions, Kant
wrote poems in honor of deceased colleagues.
Here is one composed for a Professor Lilien-
thal:
"Over what follows, life extends its shadows;
We know only what we have to do;
Death does not deprive Lilienthal of hope:
  He finally believes that he is doing right;
  And his doing makes his belief happy."

~

Which does not mean, however, that everything is henceforth

self-evident. The sublime is produced in an "aesthetic presentation," and not only by way of a discursive presentation. Doubtless, discourse is at least something that can be mastered technically: but the "sublime" style, as simple as it may be, is still something that is "added" to discourse (*pure* discourse is neither pronounced nor written). Following from this fact, sublime prose is by itself something that pure philosophical presentation cannot guarantee for itself: it is produced, it is pronounced "without intention and without art," without *Kunst*, that is, without perhaps *die schöne Kunst*, without "fine art," and therefore without poetry, and thus without artifice, *but also*, and first of all, without *technical mastery*. Discourse can be calculated and deliberated. Sublime prose should be something that shows itself and remains in its presentation, in this, exactly like the *well-armored treatise* of mathematics.

But just as much as mathematics does not deal with the existence of things—with *quid*—there is, reciprocally, no *Euclid* of philosophy. And to the "*Quid?*" that constitutes its own proper question, philosophy is obliged to attach, we remind ourselves, a Witz. As if one could not answer this question without making a joke [*faisant un mot*] and thus by exceeding sublime simplicity, in practicing art and artifice. Could there be a sublime and prosaic Witz?[9] The question is absurd, or only a Witz. Not more than, however, the demand of the system, which requires an art to inscribe its *monogram*—at the same time, with this art, it demands to infinitely transcend, and even to exclude the possibilities of art in the name of the sublime.

The *architectonic* is the name of this contradiction: it is the *art*, or the technique, of the system, the specificity of which is established precisely by means of the opposition of the organic schema (of affinity) to the schema or the procedure of *technique*.[10]

The strict purity and scholastic form in
which so many of Kant's propositions present
themselves gives to their content a hardness
and a singularly strange character; without
these veils, they appear as the out-of-date
pretensions of universal reason. I have often

remarked that philosophical truths must be found in one form and applied and developed in another. The beauty of an edifice is not visible until one has removed the mason's and carpenter's materials and taken down the scaffolding behind which the edifice rose. But most of Kant's disciples permitted themselves to take the spirit rather than the machinery of his system, revealing thereby that they resemble the worker more than the architect.
— Friedrich Schiller, *Werke und Briefe*, Letter to Prince Augustenburg, July 13, 1793

But this contradiction forms the structure and even the nature, so to speak, of the sublime. One shouldn't forget that the satisfaction of the sublime may be had only by way of the "mediation" of pain. (Is it necessary to add that this "mediation" owes nothing to Hegel") This pain stems from the constitutive failure of sublime presentation: the sublime articulates itself, on and in an inability, a radical insufficiency of the mind to present (to itself) its end. If it's possible—though it is *barely* possible—to separate hideous ugliness and monstrosity from the sublime,[11] it remains that the latter

> concerns only ideas of reason, which, though they cannot be exhibited adequately, are aroused and called to mind *by this very inadequacy* [italics mine], which can be exhibited in sensibility. (*CJ*, 99)

and that the "tension of the imagination" in inadequation—in this inadequate presentation and this inadequation rendered sensible—a violent tension "to treat nature as a schema [for ideas]" that "both repels our sensibility and yet attracts us at the same time" (*CJ*, 124).

The system, therefore, *is* not sublime: *but sublime is the terrifying inadequation of its monogram in it* (the "monogram" is the agent: we shall demonstrate this in *Kosmotheoros*). Prose *is* not sublime;

but sublime is the inadequation of its style, which is such that it overturns its simplicity outside of every style, in the account ledgers of a philosopher-shopkeeper. The writer can stand all the terror—or all the terrifying charm—of this sublimity or sublime syncope. If the philosopher tears himself away from the dangerous fascination of Isis-Medusa, it's only to fall into dread, bitterness, and the paralysis of the writer without style, always cut off from his own presentation:

> As before, the Pequod steeply leaned over
> towards the sperm whale's head, now, by the
> counterpoise of both heads, she regained her
> even keel; though sorely strained, you may
> well believe. So, when on one side you hoist
> in Locke's head, you go over that way; but
> now, on the other side, hoist in Kant's and
> you come back again; but in very poor plight.
> —Herman Melville, *Moby Dick*

The schema of the system should present itself a priori. However, it is this "a priori" that transcendental delimitation forbids a priori, which is *the same* as saying that Kant renounced the talent of this presentation, the talent of poetry as pure manifestation. The Darstellung of the system should be what one could call, by way of a painful logodaedalie, and to concentrate what Darstellung implies into a "single word," a *phenomenogram*. There is no phenomenogram—the grapheme is always inadequate, uncertain, buried, misshapen, or damaged. Even books always have printing errors. There is prose, and the book trade (the shopkeeper is perhaps a bookseller), because there is no nature—but only the inadequation between nature and second nature, or the moral law. And that is why there is no legible manifestation of the latter, no Book:

> The visitor . . . a small man scarcely five feet
> high, in an unbuttoned twill jacket with a
> white stock. . . . His hair was curled in sau-
> sages and powdered—or was it a periwig?—

and fastened behind with a gray bow. He
was in the prime of life; around his bright
vivacious eyes were crow's feet, which showed
intensive thought. . . . Breaking with his life-
long habit, he had come all the way from
Königsberg because Peter was sick. . . . "God
is dead," Peter understood him to say. Peter
sat up. "I know that," he protested. "And you
didn't say it anyway. Nietzsche did." "Yes, Nietzsche said that. And even when Nietzsche
said it, the news was not new, and maybe not
so tragic after all. . . . No, what I have to say
to you is something important . . . "Again he
looked Peter steadily and searchingly in the
eyes. "Perhaps you have guessed it. Nature is
dead, *mein kind.*" —Mary McCarthy, *Birds
of America*

~

Second nature is unable to *present itself.* However, this second
nature is the pure legality of reason, the foundation of its autonomy: *ethics* here means less a "morality" than Reason in its purest
ethos. We carry this second nature in ourselves, in an ideal manner, and it is not by any means chimerical, Kant specifies, yet

> trying to realize the ideal in an example, i.e.,
> in appearance,—as, e.g., to realize the wise
> person in a novel—is unfeasible and has,
> moreover, something preposterous and not
> very edifying about it. For in such an attempt
> the natural limits that continually impair the
> completeness in the idea make any illusion
> impossible, and the good itself that lies in the
> idea is thereby made suspect and similar to a
> mere fiction. (*CPR*, 562)

Why is the chosen example—the example of a hypothetical
moral example—that of the novel? Because philosophy is not able

to darstellen by itself the wise man as such. As we have already pointed out, it "personifies" the "ideal of the philosopher" as a *type*: in one sense, it thus does *better* than the novel; but, at the same time, it does far worse, since an ideal type is not yet a *character*. It remains the *exposition* of an idea. Permitting ourselves to play a little with language—though very little . . . —one would have to say that literature here is the ideal. Literature offers Darstellung as figuration, as the staging of a palpable character. Yet what does Kant declare? On the one hand, that the dramatization of the wise man is impractical (why? we will never learn); on the other hand, that it would be "hardly edifying" because we *could not believe in it*, we who know only too well the limits of nature. Moral literature is thus condemned as *fiction*, not because it is literature (Dichtung), but because it mimics a life that human finitude knows to be impossible to emulate. Or, rather: *literature will only come to be determined as fiction from the point of view of the philosophy that determines the ideal beyond the limits of possible experience*. One has to be able to believe in it . . . : such is the curious sigh of the philosopher in front of his own ideal, in front of literature.

This means, therefore, that "second nature" cannot be conceived as the basis of or the substitute for the first. Its character as "nature" is infinitely fleeting and fainting. "Second nature" only means inadequation itself, the impossibility inscribed in the law of reason of ever presenting itself: "radical evil" is nothing other than this, the evil that originated, let us recall, in the *narrative* of the fall of the *sublime* angel. The sublime is necessarily Luciferian—that is to say, according to an indecipherable synonymy—necessarily satanic.[12]

The sublime is thus the locus of displacement—a contradictory expression that marks the fact that this place itself is displaced. It syncopates the very principle of all presentation.

From this comes the status of "exposition"—as well as the insidious and repeated insistence of literature in philosophy. This is because the purity of prose and the absence of art cannot help but find themselves stealthily and violently, and in every case dangerously, transported toward what threatens philosophy, or toward what the prose-speaker of discourse is incapable of. In the first *Critique*, Kant can well refuse the idea of a wise man in a novel, just as he renounced, we should recall, concrete examples that are "necessary only from the popular point of view" (*CPR*, 12). This position, which is valid up to a certain point for pure theoretical reasons, no longer is so in pure practical reason (though one does not come without the other). In the latter, *practice* as such must be able to offer reason at least the staging of its own possibility. Furthermore, the moral ideal—the figure of the Human Being in general—will ceaselessly and obstinately begin to demand its own pure *literary figures* in the guise of "phenomonograms." The same goes for Jesus, the *hero* (the word is Kant's) of the popular narrative of rational religion. The same goes for the moral example in general: the good example, the one that doesn't awaken an exalted enthusiasm and which, by way of a simple refusal to lie, repeats the universal maxim itself, is given by way of a *poem* in the second *Critique*: "Juvenal presents such an example in a climax that makes the reader feel vividly the force of the incentive present in the pure law of duty, as duty":

> Esto bonus miles, tutor bonus, arbiter idem
> Integer; etc. (*CPrR*, 267)[13]

Knowing what power over Kant a quotation
from a Roman poet had always had, I simply
replied—"Post equitem sedet atra cura," and
for the present he said no more. —Thomas
De Quincey, "The Last Days of Immanuel
Kant"

Philosophical poetry, philosophy contaminated by poetry against its will, means this: the system, insofar as it involves [*comporter*] presentation—and it necessarily does so—brings about displacement [*emporte*]. One shouldn't even say *its* displacement, since displacement occurs precisely before the system is *there*, though it only takes "place" in its occurrence insofar as the system is "sketched." The Kantian sketch, the blueprint, the preliminary and rough outline without details, constitute a system with scholastic language and the lack of elegance, as we have already pointed out. The system is always there, so to speak, *in general*: which is also what renders it inadequate (to itself) and fragile from the beginning. In the preface where we started, Kant wrote that "it is enough that my work be roughly elaborated," but the difference between a "roughly outlined" system and one that is congenitally in failure, or blocked, is always at risk of evaporating.

But there's more: the system itself, to the entire extent that it constructs itself or comes about, comprises among its fundamental rules the disjunction of places, dis-placement. The Kantian unity places itself always in plurality, and within it, discourse always forbids itself from being reassimilated into a pure presence-to-self. Such is the necessary consequence of the critical principal of delimitation. That is why, for example, transcendental philosophy repeats itself or restages itself as the necessary separation of territories in his political philosophy:

> The idea of the right of nations presupposes the *separation* of many neighboring states independent of one another. And though such a condition is of itself a state of war, . . . this is nevertheless better, in accordance with the idea of reason, than the fusion of them by one overgrowing the rest and passing into a universal monarchy.[14]

Here, just as in theoretical legislation, the tracing of limits is the only guarantee against dogmatic and/or fanatic despotism. Reason thus permanently imposes, and does so upon itself, in the minimum, the power of the state of war. This war is paradoxically a wise disposition of nature. Since, says the same text:

> *nature* . . . makes use of two means to prevent peoples from intermingling and to separate them: differences of *language* and of *religion.* . . . [15]

The war that nature desires is thus the unexpected procedure by means of which it aims at peace, or harmony, that is to say, the ideal of a "second nature" as the sole and universal legislation. Everywhere, heterogeneity and conflict are inscribed in principle. Armed neighbors and border guards are the rational condition itself. Wearing armor is obligatory *not because of the reason of State* [raison d'Etat], *but by the state of reason.*

However, it is the *same* obligation and the *same* oversight that must be exercised between philosophy and poetry, as is witnessed by the long critique—turned, moreover, with the most elegant of preteritions—addressed to Herder, in the second part of the assessment that we are already familiar with. Let us be content to read a fragment on the subject:

> But just briefly we want to question whether the poetic spirit that enlivens his expression does not also sometimes intrude into the author's philosophy; whether instead of occasional neighborly excursions out of the area of the philosophical into the sphere of poetic language the limits and domains of both are not completely disarranged; whether frequently the tissue of daring metaphors, poetic images, and mythological allusions does not serve to conceal the corpus of thought as if under a hoop skirt. . . .

. . . however, just as the distinction between a "neighborly excursion" and an illegal incursion could well prove to be fragile, this criticism itself is not simple. One has to go on to finish the sentence:

> . . . instead of letting it glimmer forth agreeably as under a translucent veil.[16]

Kant also had an extraordinary imagination, part reproductive, part productive, though the latter exercising itself only in the acute comparison or in the joyous Witz, the naïve playfulness at which he showed himself to be brilliant. —Rosenkranz, *Hegel as German National-Philosopher*

It is true that this "veil"—it's the word of the translator—is also a *Gewand*, a dress or an article of clothing, but being transparent, what material would it be made out of, if not of sailcloth? It is however, *clothing*: the clothing of statues are part of the *ornament*, simultaneously both distinct and very close to the costume (*CJ*, §14), and thus to order and *elegance*. The truth (or the beauty?) of Isis is assuredly still her nudity; her "beautiful form" (*CJ*, §14) can nonetheless incorporate, in order "to be pleasing to the eyes," an article of clothing. Is it, this one, true or not? Perhaps that is not the question. One should rather ask the following one: *Why* must Isis be dressed, and in a transparent veil? Is it on the subject of the truth itself that it should be necessary "to spend fortunes of Witz" to "throw a veil" over the threat of animality? Kant is careful to only evoke a question along these lines. Let us be content, for the moment in any case, to state that it is necessary to *hide* or *favor* something, and the nudity of the goddess is perhaps comparable to the "matter roughly elaborated."

There is *also* a judicious—and philosophical—use of the veil. A use, therefore, of Witz, and of logodaedalie. *There is a capable, calculated, cautious use of the irrefutable heterogeneity itself*—for the pleasure of the *eyes* (of the theoretician). At the heart of the displacement, it is important to weave between disconnected places a light, complex network that is sometimes capable of traversing foreign and even hostile borders in order to not be swallowed by chaos. Whether this is by brusque banishment or by measured borrowings, the desire for elegance—the system's very desire—can only cut itself a labyrinthine path in the midst of ruins and traps. The system itself perhaps assumes the form of a labyrinth—inside which, in spite of everything, prose will be the Ariadne's thread, but where the labyrinth itself imposes the detours of literature. Between two logodaedalies, one has to be able to choose one, but one cannot pretend to reject both.[17] Perhaps, against Greek *daidaleos* (brilliant, worked, jeweled, artistically fashioned), it is necessary to choose the Latin *daedalus* (industrious, ingenious, capable). But one always finds the shadow of Daedalus.[18]

Kant. That which resembles the art of build-
ing labyrinths. Long circuitous routes and
tricks, etc. Hedges. Appears to make the place
seem larger by the multiple number of buildings. —Joubert, *Notebooks*

I also like a priori knowledge and a priori synthetic judgments: this is because my whole life
I had proceeded from fiction and from obser-
vation, and only then analytically. . . . But for
all that, I lacked words to speak, and had even
fewer sentences, and there, for the first time,
a theory seemed to be smiling at me. It was
its easy accessibility that I was enjoying, but
there was no way I would risk myself in the
labyrinth: I was frozen as much by the poetic
gifts as I was by the human understanding.
—Goethe, *Effects of Modern Philosophy*

> . . . as we must presuppose [a purposive ar-
> rangement of nature in a system] if we are
> to have any hope of finding our way in [the]
> labyrinth [resulting] from the diversity of
> particular laws. Hence judgment itself makes
> a priori the technic of nature [a] principle for
> its reflection. (*CJ*, 402)

The assumption of the unity of the system based on a technique
borrowed from the *idea* of nature—a technique of judgment that
operates "in the manner of art"—guides the thinker inside the
labyrinth. It is not possible to come out of this labyrinth—because
of the character of the assumption itself, because of the *artifact*
that constitutes the Ariadne thread—in order to see its entirety
from above. Mazes are not only the constraint that results from
displacement; the labyrinthine procedure is also the only art or
artifice that allows one to orient oneself. One cannot escape from
the labyrinth, but inside, it is only by way of a certain art that one
achieves specifically the sublime "without intention and without

art." In the mazes of literature, there is no way to not weave prose. When Bouterwerk, the *Poet*, announces to Kant his intention to give courses on the *Critique*, Kant responds in the following way:

> The glad and spirited temper with which your poems have often delighted me did not prepare me to expect that dry speculation might also be a stimulus for you. But speculation invariably leads to a certain sublimity, the sublimity of the Idea, which can draw the imagination into play and produce useful analogies, though of course the Idea cannot actually be reached this way. (*C*, 461)

Bouterwerk could also be the one, the writer wished for by the preface of the first *Critique*:

> These worthy men have that happy combination of thorough insight with a poetic talent for lucid exposition, the very talent that I am not aware of in myself. . . . (*CPR*, 39)

Certainly, Kant had the rare good fortune to act on a stage hardly lacking in trimmings and a wall of heads against which the accents of his lyre reverberated more clearly and resoundingly, just as the Ancients packed their theaters with empty pots in order to reinforce the resonance of the actors' voices. —Jean Paul, *The Life of Fixlein*

～

Yet the poet, the one who "ventures to give sensible expression to rational ideas of invisible beings" (*CJ*, 183), is at the same time the one who defines and exemplifies (though here, the two operations more or less overlap) the *genius*. To the *brain* that Newton was are opposed the *geniuses* of Homer and Wieland. And genius, we know, is the man of "true popularity" (*CJ*, §47).

However, just what Kant really understands—if one can speak here of justice at all—by "genius" is what must be discovered along the way in a singular labyrinth. One can only get a glimpse of something by pursuing several separate paths, though they all crisscross as a kind of still-undrafted text. Here, the evidence consists only of indices, tortuous, dispersed paths along which one grows weary—along which everything happens as if Kant himself, the writer *and* the philosopher, grew exhausted or *engineered* to simultaneously multiply and muddy the traces of genius.

One could, for example, attempt to untangle the double opposition between the presentation by *method* (*modus logicus*) and the presentation by *manner* (*modus aestheticus*) at the end of the analysis of genius *and* of the two together in relation to mannerism (*CJ*, 187). Since, when Kant writes "in art a product is called *mannered* only if the way the artist conveys his idea *aims* at singularity and is not adequate to the idea" (*CJ*, 187), we must understand, as if from a surprising indecision of the text, that the hypothesis of a work that combines manner and method is not excluded. Of course, this means first of all that true artistic genius presents the Ideas of reason through its art, but this can also mean that nothing forbids the philosopher from *also* putting to work the *modus aestheticus*.

However, we shall devote ourselves to the presentation of the models of genius that takes place in the *Anthropology from a Pragmatic Point of View*. When this work repeats the analysis of genius in the third *Critique*, it turns out that Newton is no longer a *brain*, but rather a *genius*, henceforth associated with Leibniz. Together, they have the general characteristics of genius without a single poet being opposed to them (*CJ*, §59). Kant's two models, which are also two "rivals," the mathematician and the philosopher, are geniuses, are even *genius* exemplified. (And let's not forget that Hume, for his part, is at the very least a model of style . . .). However, we know from the third *Critique* that there is no exemplary relation except between one genius and another. Kant is therefore a genius: the result appears self-evident. Yet once again, it is not as simple as that. After he designates this double model of ingenuity in general, Kant only mentions one type of genius in particular:

> The *architectonic mind,* which methodically
> examines the connection of all the sciences
> and how they support one another, is only
> a subordinate type of genius, but still not a
> common one. (*A,* 122)

Perhaps this text more than any other allows one to mercilessly
condemn all the vulgar mistakes that accumulate in the rush to
tie a text to the individual who wrote it, clutch at all its supposed
winks or extract confessions. Evidently, the one who thus designates himself a "subaltern genius" is Kant. But at the same time,
it's not Kant, if "Kant" will have to be thought as the author of his
own presentation. Because this last one is precisely the one that
fails him, and assigns him his "subaltern" place. What is designated
in this last sentence is something that probably never signs itself
except with the name of an author because it is the question of the
author that is at stake in it, that is, the question of the impossible
"self" of Darstellung. The "subaltern genius" is the signature, for
the one who "holds forth" [*qui « tient » un discours*], of the impossibility of mastering the ideal conditions that discourse itself imposes on its own production and its own refinement [*tenue*]. The
"architectonic mind" grasps the interrelationship of the sciences,
it does not produce them (and that is the general condition that
Critique establishes from the very beginning for philosophy: the
latter does not produce the sciences, it receives them). Its "genius"
thus signs the impossibility of being the author, the Dichter, of a
presentation, and simultaneously, the impossibility of there being
a Darstellung without an author, of there being a pure autopresen-
tation of the system. Kant signs the impossibility of designating in
Kant the *true* genius—but also the need for making "Kant" *nearly*
a genius. The kant ingeniously undecides itself.

This is also why the "question" of the author or of the genius of
philosophy does not arise as such and in fact is eluded by way of
the compromise implicit in this sentence: in question is precisely
what Kant will not have been able to elaborate as a philosophical
question. The four famous Kantian questions are always lacking

the fifth, which consequently haunts all his texts as a test, as their test and their putting-to-the-test: *How to present philosophy?*

The architectonic is the art of systems, but art does not present the system—the presentation of which should be sublime and without art. The architectonic does not arrive at *its ends*. It's not that philosophy would be incapable of thinking art, the literary art of exposition. On the contrary, it thinks it and puts it in its place without fail. But what it thinks in thinking it—in producing the categories of "literature" and of "genius"—is the inadequation and the displacement of its own thought insofar as this thought, this *critical* thought, chose itself to be [*s'est décidée*] the thought of its own delimitation and thus its own exposition. Ultimately, this thought should have been nothing other than philosophy as the thought of its own literature—that is to say, of all the *remains* that pure thought excluded. ("Thought" should not be understood here in any sense other than a Kantian one: "Thinking is an act which consists in referring an object to a given intuition"; literary *aesthetics* should be the intuition referring to the object "philosophy").

Therefore, the *modest* results of this test [*épreuve*] of reason— that is to say, this "proof" [*preuve*] of inadequation thought (the sublime system) which can only "be" the inadequation in thinking, or which produces the doctrine of the inadequate *being of* and *for* (a) being-thought [*l'être inadequate* de *et à l'être-pensé*] ("the proud name of an *ontology* . . . must give way for the modest name of a mere analytic . . . ")—this test of thinking, therefore, was left to the *subaltern genius* to present the *modest* results of.[19] Yet by the same token, it's left to "Kant-the-writer" to mark its trace. Kant-the-writer is the problem or the test of Kant-the-philosopher; at the same time, it is its means, which allows him to hope that philosophy manages to present itself. The kant-writer is thus what is most properly the "genius" in the "subaltern genius."

However, Kant gathered identifications of the philosopher (the philosopher-writer) and the genius in his notes. For example, this note between 1765 and 1773:

> The philosophical *esprit* is original and there-
> fore genius (because original is not simply
> what is unique, but rather that which is not
> an *ectype*.)[20]

(If the philosophical genius is not, for all that, the supersensible
archtypon, he is then the *type*, that is to say, the practical figure of
the schema or the monogram.) —Or this other note:

> There is a kind of philosophical exposition
> the power of which makes itself felt nearly
> right away in school, but its whole influence
> is limited to a virile use of reason. The other
> kind has no power of its own in the school,
> but has all the more influence in life. To the
> first belongs the mechanistic, to the second
> the culture of genius.[21]

—Or still this one, which can be read between its lines if one re-
members that critique consists in drawing from the pure sources
of reason:

> Genius derives its product from the
> sources. . . . The arts of industry recognize an
> example and need it; those of genius are cre-
> ative, that is, they proceed in accordance with
> an idea. The power of judgment and taste de-
> termine the limits of genius, hence without
> these genius borders on madness. In the art
> of poetry genius has its true field, because to
> poetize [*dichten*] is to create. (*NF*, 504)

(In 1802, Hegel criticizes Schulze, an enemy
of Kant. This author recognizes "with the
greatest respect" that the *Critique* owes nothing to *genius*, nor to luck, but all to the sole
power of thought. Hegel replies:

"The contempt for genius and for the great
gifts of nature, the opinion according to

which imagination (*Phantasie*) would lend
the exposition of philosophy only the flowers
of eloquence, and that reason would invent
(*dichten*)—nearly in the sense of the lies the
newspapers invent daily—or rather, when it
would produce its inventions (*erdichten*) on
the far side of common reality, it would only
produce chimeras, extravagances, theosophi-
cal caprices, so that it could still surpass the
imagination in invention, even when the
latter invents in its highest flights—we can't
say which is victorious, the barbarism or the
naiveté with which the absence of genius is
praised, or the triviality of concepts.") —
Hegel, *Relation of Skepticism to Philosophy*

. . . But Kant never carried over or copied his notes into his
philosophical writings. It is as if, at the same time that he made
use of a certain talent, it was necessary to renounce philosophical
ingenuity (its use? its title?). And just as in the decision that concerns talent, one can see this "sacrifice" form and reform the undecidability of (Kant's) genius. Let us say that "genius" is the word
for the production of the indeterminable in philosophy, for this
pure autoproduction incapable of autoproducing itself by itself,
producing in spite of everything this incapacity *itself*, and invali-
dating the purity of this production in the same stroke.

In effect, in a general way, it is the sacrifice of genius that prescribes the third *Critique* (§50): in the presence of a conflict between genius and taste (which, too, arises from judgment and constitutes the *discipline* of genius), if "something has to be sacrificed,
then it should rather be on the side of genius" (*CJ*, 188). (It is
probably necessary, we know, to avoid madness, the contamination of madness.) The problems of "Kant-the-writer," the question
of philosophical exposition endlessly taken up again and again,
derive from this sacrifice. A sacrifice that nonetheless cannot be a
simple and pure abandonment. It leaves obscure, confused traces,

but at the same time, as we shall see, ones that are excessive, unbearable.

⌒

The genius, who is characterized, first of all, externally at least, by his difference from the "spirit of imitation" and from the pedagogical relation in general, belongs to a series of terms—talent, Witz, and judgment—that we are already familiar with. He crowns and exceeds it: he constitutes in some way the vanishing point of this series of terms, the multiplicity of which, the exchanges and displacements of which, corresponds in fact to the explosion or the blurring of an obscure and central point (where every *center* is ruined): the point where Darstellung and Dichtung cross—partitioned, combined, undecidable—the punctuality of a pure source always in itself confronted by a necessary heterogeneity, the point—or the *syncope*—of a virginity crossed by sexual difference, the unsettled point where *the* philosopher "with a virile use of reason," would be unable to couple with a feminine, elegant, popular habit of reason. The genius, the philosopher *himself*, undecides himself at this point.

The critique of *pure* reason delimits the regions and the regimes of the exercise of reason, puts an end to every one of its pretensions or needs by way of a determinate legislation: but in doing so, it also always delimits the *purity* of the critical instance itself, of this tribunal or of this relation of reason to itself, a relation that is pure *and* productive, and which constitutes, as we know, the point of its *immaculate conception*.

However, although the immaculate conception *conceives* the pure respect of reason for its own law, it is itself *inconceivable* for reason. To think that one could present it would be to conceive it like the "philosopher's stone" the adepts of which fell into "leaps of genius" (*CprR*, 270). The genius of rational autonomy always risks presenting himself with this stone—a statue of Isis or a face that turns one into stone. The immaculate conception is a Medusa as much as it is a Virgin.

I would open the reader's eye, that he might
see—hosts of intuitions ascending to the fir-
mament of pure understanding, and hosts of
concepts descending into the deep abyss of
the most palpable sensibility, on a ladder of
which no sleeper has yet dreamt—and the
dancing procession of these *Mahanaim* or
two hosts of reason—the secret and vexatious
Chronicle of their love-affair and rape—and
the entire theogony of all forms of giants and
heroes of the Sulammite and Muse, in the
mythology of light and darkness—down to
the play on forms that an old *Baubo carries
on with herself—inaudita specie solaminis*, as
St. Arnobius says—and of a new *immaculate virgin*, who however may not become a
mother of God, for which St. Anselm takes
her. —J. G. Hamann, *Metacritique of the Pur-
ism of Reason*[22]

The moment in which philosophy conceives its immaculate
conception is precisely the moment in which it tears itself apart,
or remains transfixed, torn between an inconceivable virginity and
the terrifying presentation of an intolerable face that castrates the
philosopher or leaves him to die of laughter in front of the abyss of
his own mutilation. The moment of critique is the one in which
philosophy—in thinking for the first time its *pure* determination
as *reason*—confronts this intolerable displacement. It confronts
it without knowing it—without, in any case, the *knowledge* prescribed by its discourse. This is why all that remains in philosophy
is its *cant*, in other words, the confused and fragmentary exposition, simultaneously aesthetic and moral, of an obscure problem,
seemingly marginal, of "literature" in "philosophy." Simultaneously raised and evaded, this problem also constitutes the mask
of the intolerable in reason—or sets the standard for what Kant
could not and perhaps did not want to know about.

At the end of the North, there was once a
bizarre and powerful creature. A man? No,

a system, a living scholasticism, bristling,
hard, a rock, a stone cut to the sharpness of
a diamond in the granite regions of the Bal-
tic. All religion, all philosophy, had arrived
there, only to be shattered. And he, immu-
table. No grasp on the external world. He
was called Immanuel Kant; he called himself
Critique. . . . He was followed, seen walking
West, along the road that brought mail from
France. . . .

O humanity . . . to see Kant stir, grow wor-
ried, and set out on the road, like a woman,
in search of news. . . . " —Jules Michelet,
History of the French Revolution

Talent, Witz, and judgment (Mutterwitz) constitute the critical
instance of reason, and totter from the effects of its displacement.
The genius summarizes and repeats this trembling. He is himself
the loss of measure, a disproportion:

> . . . if none of the mental predispositions
> stands out beyond the proportion that is
> required for someone to constitute merely a
> person free from defects, then we must not
> expect in him any degree of what we call *ge-
> nius*; in the case of genius nature seems to de-
> part from the proportions it usually imparts
> to our mental powers, instead favoring just
> one. (*CJ*, 83, n. 57)

It's most likely by its disproportion that the genius is able to
present sublime inadequation—the only presentation that could
be "adequate" to the system. And yet, it's because of this disproportion—and its dangerous proximity to caricature, or to madness—that one must always be ready to sacrifice it. Or even, it's
because of ingenious disproportion that the thought of ingenuity
in the system (of the ingenuity of the *author*, of the *artist* of the
system) must forge for itself the notion, *in truth untenable*, of a
"subaltern though hardly common genius." With this brand of

monstrous or ridiculous bourgeoisie of genius, in order to avoid the precipice of madness, or of Baubo, the philosopher seems to throw himself into the arms of Monsieur Homais—a direction, in effect, frequently taken by Kant's style, taste, and sentences.[23] As if, renewing "popular philosophy" in part from elsewhere, Kant had *also* given philosophical letters of credit to *literature* in the sense that, very quickly, both "philosophers" *and* "writers" will grow suspicious and contemptuous. Flaubert, Baudelaire, Mallarmé, or Proust will detest *literature*, that is to say, the philosophical product of the renunciation of a reason that is unbearable:

> Whatever the theosophical coffeehouses and the Kantian beer-cellars may say, we are deplorably ignorant of the nature of the Good. I myself who, without wishing to boast, have lectured at my pupils, in all innocence, on the philosophy of the aforesaid Immanuel Kant, can see no precise directive for the case of the social casuistry with which I am now confronted by that *Critique of Practical Reason* in which the great unfrocked priest of Protestantism Platonized in the Teutonic manner for a prehistorically sentimental and aulic Germany, in the obscure interests of a Pomeranian mysticism. It's the *Symposium* once again, but held this time in Königsberg, in the local style, indigestible and chaste, and reeking of sauerkraut and without any young gigolos around. —Marcel Proust, *The Captive*[24]

One will rightly object that the "subaltern genius" is no less a genius and that he is above "average"; furthermore, one can comment on the bad faith or the false modesty of the formula. The philosopher is a genius (and thus an artist): this is *also* (almost) readily legible in Kant. But what is also legible, inevitably, is the unnerving proximity of genius and abnormality. The passage that is concerned with the disproportion of genius also contains, without any qualifications, the following lines:

> . . . if what is characteristic in this way is
> exaggerated, that is, if it offends against the
> standard idea (of the purposiveness of the
> kind) itself, then it is called a *caricature*. Ex-
> perience shows, moreover, that such wholly
> regular faces usually indicate that inwardly
> too the person is only mediocre. (*CJ*, 83, n.
> 57)

The sublime simplicity of prose could easily brush up against
the grotesque. The *type* of the philosopher (or the wise man) dif-
fers from caricature (from *his* caricature) only by an infinitesimal
difference that separates "exaggeration" from "disproportion": an
inappreciable, fleeting difference that probably nearly always permits mistaking one for the other, or both at the same time. An
undecidable function inscribes the same silhouette on one and the
other. In spite of this, one can probably distinguish between them:
in the "Characteristic" of the *Anthropology*, after having once more
insisted on the relation between the regularity of facial traits and
mediocrity, Kant defines caricature as "the intentionally exaggerated sketch (a distortion) of the face in affect, devised for derision
and belonging to mimicry" (*A*, 200). Further on, we learn that this
mimicry "translates the impression of an emotion . . . by the pains-
taking restraint in gesture or in tone itself" from which it is difficult to remove oneself when one is moved (*A*, 200). The mimic
belongs to the order of affect and tone and, therefore, to the order
of pathological danger in general. The opposite of caricature is a
face that "has been *disfigured* and made unpleasing because of the
coloring of his skin or pockmarks" and which "has lost its charm,"
but which can be redeemed by the expression of benevolence and
moral force (*A*, 200).

> It must rather be included among a variety
> that lies in nature and must not be called a
> distorted face (which would be repulsive); for
> even if it is not lovely, it can inspire love, and
> although it is without beauty, it is still not
> ugly. (*A*, 200)

Although this is the portrait of a wise man more than of a genius, although the genius surely demands some additional disproportion that probably renders him less easy to make out than a caricature, one has to admit that this face *without art* is the sublime face of the writer of philosophical prose. It can be taken for a grotesque and terrifying mask, but one does not *have to* do so—which supposes that one has to vanquish a certain fear in order to unmask it. And this fear is due to the traces of an anomaly or an illness. The genius, or the philosopher, inevitably arises out of the pathological. The ugliness of Socrates is here no longer the deceptive appearance that conceals a virtuous soul. In the thinking of the phenomena, appearance is exposition based in sensible form: that of the philosopher—or the writer—seems destined to deformity. Logodaedalus is sick.

The last work published by Kant (in 1798, along with the *Anthropology*), *The Conflict of the Faculties*, ends with the "Conflict of the 'faculty of philosophy' with the 'faculty of medicine.'" This section contains, in the guise of a response to Hufeland, the author of a *Macrobiotics*, the "art of prolonging life," Kant's own discourse on long life, to the extent that philosophy should be able to remedy the frailties of age (of the old age that bears a part of the responsibility for the *Critique*'s lack of elegance).

The first of these frailties consists of "hypochondria," a "kind of madness at the foundation of which there could very well be some sort of unhealthy condition (such as flatulence or constipation) that may be the source of it, this state is not felt immediately . . . but is misrepresented as impending illness by the inventive imagination" (*CF*, 318). The *Anthropology* (§50) develops the analysis of this madness, considered to be a "madness of chimeras" and of the imagination (an illness of genius?), which feeds on the "anxious and infantile fear at the thought of death" (fear of Isis-Medusa?), even as it is marked by a brusque alternation of humors in which the patient passes from anxiety to laughter to the Witz. (Thus, one must add that that hypochondria is, in fact, analogous to health: this is because in order to maintain one's health, one is obligated to pass periodically through the convulsions of laugh-

ter. We shall return to this.)—In its difference from other forms
of "madness," which possess an "essential and incurable" disorder
(that we shall have to analyze elsewhere), hypochondria is an "illness of the mind" that has not truly tipped over into madness; it
is in some sense an illness in health that touches in an ambivalent
way (and by imagination and Witz), both positive and negative,
on the faculties of reason. In the *Conflict of the Faculties*, it defines
the fundamental weakness that one has to remedy by will, by a
"firm decision" and an "effort of the mind." Yet, it is the illness of
an author, because "for me," says Kant:

> I myself have a natural disposition to hypo-
> chondria because of my flat and narrow chest,
> which leaves little room for the movement of
> the heart and lungs, and in my earlier years
> this disposition made me almost weary of life.
> (*CF*, 318)

Although Kant's illness is not an "essential disorder," it remains
to a certain extent incurable—to the extent probably that it is the
fact of a "natural disposition," similar in this to reason's irrepress-
ible dialectical illusions, or to the radical evil of human nature.
Moreover, it cannot be cured, only controlled and regulated—like
the Witz of reason. All the decisions taken, all the remedies indicated, will be able to do nothing, at the end of the work, at the
end of Kant's thought, against an inexorable attrition. This attrition is not that of Kant's discourse, nor of his body: it wears down
both at the same time (though what is *time* here? as we shall see,
it's the time of the system, the moment of synthesis). It is the attrition of the philosopher's *flesh*, if one may here be permitted to
inscribe this word under the banner of undecidability: this *flesh*
is undecidably the life *and* the theory of the philosopher, or the
chiasmus by means of which these two undecide themselves. The
philosopher remains decided on living: it's the victory of his ethic
over hypochondria—but by way of a "vegetative life." This is the
ineluctable illness of his flesh. So it goes, especially since the "ef-

fort of the mind" can no longer be a remedy. There is no longer a philosophical palliative.

A final illness left Kant feeling "disorganized—or at least weakened and dulled—in my intellectual work" (*CF*, 325). And in these pages, the ultimate appendix to the "system," where for the first time a morbid biographical concern—that nonetheless so resembles the complaints of the *writer*—becomes the pretext *or the text* of a final theoretical presentation, we learn that *the inevitable illness of the philosopher is due precisely to philosophical exposition.* This "last illness" is "an epidemic of catarrh accompanied by *distress in the head*" (the cold is Kant's perennial illness, as we shall see) (*CF*, 325). The result is that there are moments when one loses one's "presence of mind"—a kind of syncope. Against this distressing feeling, "which one can guard against in writing, though only with great labor (especially in philosophical writing, where it is not always easy to look back to one's starting point), but despite all one's efforts, one can never obviate it completely" (*CF*, 325). The syncope thus attains to philosophy as such, and it does so because it's hard to turn around and go back. Is it on account of the distance of the journey? The responsibility falls then on *discourse* itself; but isn't it also because "the point of departure" is impossible to see, or unbearable? And in turning around one would risk the fate of the wife of Lot, or that of Eurydice?—In any event, Kant reveals at this moment that philosophical armor was faulty in principle, and consequently impossible to repair, since, he continues:

> It is different with the mathematician, who can hold his concepts or their substitutes (symbols of quantity or number) before him in intuition and assure himself that, as far as he has gone, everything is correct. But the worker in the field of philosophy, especially pure philosophy (logic and metaphysics), must hold his object hanging in midair before him, and must always describe and examine it, not merely part by part, but within the totality of a system as well (the system

of pure reason). Hence it is not surprising if
metaphysicians are incapacitated sooner than
scholars in other fields or in applied philosophy. (*CF*, 325)

Thus, it is the *presentation* of the *system* that makes one sick. For
lack of the ability to be a poet (for want of either the right or the
capacity, or both), *philosophical genius necessarily disables itself.*

Without question, it is perhaps impossible to read without feeling ill this text in which the determinations of the system itself
have become the practical conditions of the work of a metaphysician who strongly resembles, in his curious acrobatics, his own
caricature. But neither does one look upon the feeling of illness
imposed on the reader by this old man and his entire work without astonishment—and probably not without some fear—as he
struggled and exhausted himself, through some formidable and
miserable mazes, *to write*, perhaps for the first time in history, *pure
philosophy.*

I only want to remind you that an irrevocable
engagement of thought with *form* daily gives
literature its breath. In the domain of the
sensible, this engagement is the very condition of poetry; in the domain of ideas, it is
called *tone*; as surely as Nietzsche belongs to
literature, Kant does not. —Julien Gracq, *La
littérature à l'estomac*

To write pure philosophy means: *to write*—and in this sense
implies an irrevocable engagement of thought with form, of philosophy with literature, but that means: to write *in not writing*,
and that an ineluctable disengagement of thought not in relation
to "form," which would be extrinsic to it, but in regards to its own
form, *in relation to its own presentation*. At least once—though
once more in a footnote—Kant formally wrote:

Philosophy is to be considered here as the genius of reason (*Vernunft-genius*).[25]

—But reason cannot present *itself* as a genius without clouding or muddying its purity, without foundering in its own presentation, making itself mad, or disabling itself.

That is why, in the guise of an epilogue, an epitaph, or an epigram at the end of his autology, this genius of reason will conclude *The Conflict of the Faculties* with a postscript criticizing the printers of his time, who do not sufficiently protect the eyes of readers, especially since, like Kant, they are subject to a recurring "pathological condition of the eyes," to visual syncopes at the event of which, "when I am reading, a certain brightness suddenly spreads over the page, confusing and mixing up all the letters until they are completely illegible" (*CF*, 327).

> Perhaps it was those magnificent and tragic sunsets that inspired the Koenigsberg recluse philosopher Wolfgang Meynert to write his monumental *Untergang der Menschheit* (*Decline of Mankind*). We can vividly picture him pacing the seashore, bare-headed in a flowing cloak, staring with fascinated eyes at that flood of fire and blood filling more than half the sky. "Yes," he whispers in an ecstasy, "yes, the time has come to write the epilogue to the history of mankind!" And so he sat down and wrote it.[26]

~

In the *Opus postumum* one finds a project for a *preface* in which the author would have declared (had he ever finished it) that he was presenting philosophy in a "simple and unitary" exposition "that is, as a system prescribed by pure reason, not one conceived arbitrarily."[27] This preface would have cancelled the faults as well as the desires that the *preface* to the first *Critique* exhausted itself enumerating.

Yet Kant never achieved the sublime simplicity of prose. In rejecting style, he doubtless rejects—or creates—style "in the current acoustic-decorative acceptation of the term," as Borges says.[28] He thus perhaps inaugurates *into philosophy* an exhausting writing—that one is tempted to call writing *itself*, that is, the one in which, according to Borges, "the crudeness of a sentence is just as indifferent to authentic literature as its grace."[29]

However, it is also the case that Kant poses the question of literature in philosophy only insofar as it is a question of *his* literature, and thus of a "literature" that figures the property of, the beauty proper to, and even the truth of . . . Truth. (And it's not certain that it is not *still* what Borges, too, Borges-the-philosopher in any case, understands when he says "*authentic* literature.") Kant discovers and gives rise to the desire for an elegance sacrificed: as a result, he remains tied to this desire, the captive of his "object." In other words, perhaps not exactly of Dichtung, but of Darstellung itself, or the *will* to Darstellung. The philosophy of kant, in fact, says two things at once: "It is important to separate what can appear to me from what is in itself"; it also says, "What is in itself must appear to me in one way or another." This equivocation (to borrow the term used by Gérard Granel) has engendered both Romantic philosophy and Hegel, both Nietzsche and phenomenology.[30] However, in both cases (in other words, as is evident, in cases that add up to the quasitotality of modern history of philosophy . . .), it has engendered an opposition between "pure" philosophy and "literature" that is simultaneously muddled and hardened—which for its part and as a result, can never be "pure," but designates the ambiguous realm where one finds, according to various tastes and criteria, *all the rest* of purity: in one moment bad philosophy, in the next bad literature.

It is that kant, when it declares that the thing must appear to me *in one manner or another*, engenders precisely this category of *manner*, of the *modus aestheticus*, of elegance: elegance is the concept of a "manner" that can take place in an a priori presentation excluded and relegated to mathematical ideality. As a result it is the concept without concept, the diffuse and misshapen notion that receives the protean name of "literature." *Logodaedalus remains caught in the trap of presentation that he constructed.* There, he loses his energy, including his powers of thought. But something remains from his exhaustion, indefinitely, some Dichtung perhaps or at least some writing that, without any poetry, any elegance, will ceaselessly wear him out.

Some student was very loudly tapping his fingers on his bench.

"Young man!"

Professor Cripure weighed his chances and stared hard at the little rascal, who was crumpled over with laughter.

"What do you have to say for yourself, Mr. Gentric?"

"Is it true, sir, that Immanuel Kant, the immortal author of the *Cripure* of Pure Reason . . . "

A pure frenzy took hold of the class. They no longer contented themselves with laughing; they clapped their hands, tapped their feet under tables, and screamed "Crip . . . crip . . . Cripure . . . "

Cripure closed his eyes.

"Is it true he was a virgin?" finished Gentric. —Louis Guilloux, *Le Sang Noir*

§ 7 Logodaedalus

What does it mean to say that philosophy is exhausting itself? That it has quickly arrived at the bottom? Perhaps. That it is exhausting, and thus unable to be completed, or to complete its foundation? Probably this, too. Or, at least—if this is a "least"—that one arrives at it only at the price of an irreparable fatigue and a lethal syncope? One has to grant this as well. But what is death?

Or rather, between life and death, is it the price of an ill-health that must be paid? Perhaps even this. What, then, is a *living death*? What are the last days of Immanuel Kant, when it is no longer possible to decide between his life and his death, his thought and his stupefaction, when the name of Kant marks itself as its own undecidability? This author's *Critique*, the *Critique* which he did not succeed in becoming the author of, seeks elegance and pleasure: but such as it is written, such as it is not written, it is austere and cold, prosaic and insensitive—and "the void of sensations we perceive in ourselves arouses a horror (*horror vacui*) and, as it were, the presentiment of a slow death which is regarded as more painful than when fate suddenly cuts the thread of life" (*A*, 129).

However, it can also be the case that the price is still more miniscule. Which would mean in the circumstances only more difficult, more exhausting to calculate, even if it were only the price of simple mockery, in other words almost nothing in the eyes of theory, in the eyes of the critical and architectonic project and its formidable consequences in the history of philosophy. This monumental enterprise—nothing less than the taking apart of the monument of metaphysics, its dismantlement, transport, and reconstruction according to a still unpublished (perhaps also unwritten) blueprint—would have simply paid for itself with a bit of ridicule? Yet at the same time, it's a question of a bit of obstinate, tortuous mockery that pervades every room and every labyrinth of the monument.

The philosopher likely placed himself on guard by admitting in advance the abjection of his style. And if he did so in several ways, since he thereby parried literary reproaches, he also thereby prepared the way for the recognition of the beauty of his style. Turned to stone by Medusa, one can nonetheless wish to exhibit oneself—perhaps one only ever exhibits oneself in stone, and not without counting on becoming oneself a Medusa. Perhaps Kant thought that the sublime of the *Critique* lies in that it takes your breath away. Is Kant's style beautiful? Who will deny that the Gorgon is beautiful? In its *own way*, as we say (*modus fascinans*). . . .

Truly profound and abstruse philosophy also has its own ways to attain the lofty peak of great diction. Where theory proceeds from a genuinely creative intellect, the intrinsic quality and even the conclusiveness of the concepts involved impart to language a loftiness suitably corresponding to inner profundity. A configuration of philosophical style of quite peculiar beauty is also found in the pursuit of abstract concepts in Fichte's and Schelling's writings; in isolated but truly gripping instances, it is found in the writings of Kant as well. —Wilhelm von Humboldt, *The Character of Languages*

. . . in the undecidable manner of the sublime, which is to no longer have any manner and yet to twist the simplicity of style on the impossibility of its exhibition, of its Darstellung. The result of this is an exhaustion from twisting oneself, to the laughter of the philosopher, that is to say (the ultimate precaution taken by Kant) to the laughter of *this* philosopher, the one who exhibited himself so that his literary *character*, by turns buffoon, clown, or old fogy, and even capable of moving you, could never again be mistaken for philosophy—which never presents itself. In the final analysis, the whole "literary" problem of the philosopher, and perhaps all of literature, preserves the archetype of the Philosopher *such as he-in-himself* [tel qu'en lui-même] *presents himself to himself alone (to whom, then?).*[1]

In a certain *manner*, therefore, it's still Kant who signed his own literary dramas, always he who sketched these portraits and who subscribes to the propositions therein about philosophy, about its flair and its style.

But in the *same manner*, this defense exhibited the gap in his armor. The philosopher who multiplies caricatures of his role also reveals the *inadequation between the philosopher and the Philosopher*. In philosophy, this inadequation is immemorial, and it constitutes the word "philo-sophy." Metaphysical *thinking* consists in closing the gap therein. Metaphysical *kant* consists in *thinking this thought even as literature* (as "prose," for example), thus still and always as inadequation: *the same becomes equal to itself in inscribing this proposition itself as being undecidable in the system.* It's over this impossible demonstration that the system vacillates, worries over a detail, or seeks elegance. Literary elegance can take the place of the undecidable proposition, since literature, too, is indemonstrable and irrefutable. And yet, it is not the *same* undecidability, or rather, mathematics and literature are the same which undecides itself.

This is also the reason why the mockery is insistent and why philosophy will always be identified with the Philosopher, that is to say, with the dusty and abstruse old fogy disparaged by so many latter-day hacks. The philosopher himself posed for this portrait—but it's also the only one that he can present to himself. In laughing at himself, the philosopher protects *and presents* himself. A laugh perhaps always allows something to escape that is on par with what it is protecting and holding back.

Kant, judging by his portraits, looks like an
herbalist. —Valéry, *Notebooks*

~

So it goes with the laughter of Kant-Logodaedalus, with the
theory of laughter and *theoretical laughter* such as they are found
imbricated in him. It is necessary to pause once more over this
theoretical knot—or over this syncope. It completes, in a long
"Remark," the analytic of the sublime (§54).

At this place in the text, it is a matter of distinguishing between
pleasure (*Vergnügen*), always physical, and that-which-pleases-rea-
son (*gefallen*). But it is a matter of distinguishing them in order to
better relate one to the other: pleasure and gratification (let us thus
call them) are related in philosophy and elsewhere: since it happens that "gratification (even if its cause happens to lie in ideas)
seems always to consist in a feeling that a person's life is being
furthered generally" (*CJ*, 201). Philosophy is a pleasure (as much as
it is an illness), or there is some pleasure in philosophy: in effect,
states the introduction, there is a pleasure that is proper to knowledge, an archaic pleasure, today barely noticed, yet indispensable.
Cognitive activity would be unimaginable without the impulse of
this pleasure, without its agitation—though it escapes, in cognition, the order of understanding properly speaking.

Yet what theoretical pleasure is to rational thinking, laughter
is to thought in general (and thus laughter is thus, strictly speaking, doubly valuable for cognition). Laughter gives no pleasure to
knowledge, no more so than music. Laughter is rather the trembling in which it can feel its life:

> It is not our judging of the harmony we find
> in tones or in flashes of wit—this harmony,
> with its beauty, merely serves as a necessary
> vehicle—but the furtherance of the vital pro-
> cesses of the body, the affect that agitates the
> intestines and the diaphragm, in a word the
> feeling of health (which we cannot feel with-

> out prompting), which constitutes the grati-
> fication . . . the understanding, failing to find
> what it expected, suddenly relaxes, so that we
> feel the effect of this slackening in the body
> by the vibration of our organs. . . . (*CJ*, 203)

Laughter exceeds judgment and beauty; it rests on the inadequation of a presentation (and on the "worst" one—the one that does
not present anything); it is of the order of the sublime (laughter
and the sublime are undecidably the same). Just as pain is necessary to the sublime, the "shaking" of laughter is "salutary," con-
vulsion is necessary for health. The effect of laughter is not only
comparable to, but materially identical to the effect—which Kant
analyzes elsewhere—of *sneezing*.[2]

> My bedroom overlooks a shabby living room
> in which furniture from the beginning of the
> previous century has nearly finished turning
> to dust. In the fracas coming from the ceiling,
> it seemed there was the sound of a sneeze. I
> got up to go turn out the light, I was naked
> and I paused before opening . . .
> . . . I was certain of having found Imman-
> uel Kant, who was waiting for me behind the
> door. He no longer had the diaphanous face
> that so set him apart during his life. He had
> the hirsute appearance of an unkempt young
> man wearing a three-cornered hat. I opened
> the door, and to my surprise, I found myself
> in front of emptiness. I was alone and naked
> under the fiercest rolls of thunder that I had
> ever heard. —Georges Bataille, *The Abbé C.*

Yet at the same time, health—or more specifically, the feeling of
being alive, consciousness—is only acquired or secured by a moment of syncope. Laughter is able to guarantee the condition of
possibility of gratification (consciousness *for* reason) only by a loss
in pleasure, by the syncope *of* pleasure itself. This trembling or this
agitation does not exactly allow itself to be identified with the con-

tinuous and progressive oscillation of a discourse machine: rather, it uninsures itself—and laughter communicates (?) [*sic*] with literature. (If autoeroticism is constitutive of or figures metaphysical autology, it would be necessary to say that the *auto* simultaneously breaks itself off and starts off again in Kantian laughter, that an *other* shows up there, which is not necessarily the other sex, but perhaps the same that undecides itself, ambivalent, or turned to stone, or both at once, turned to stone by itself and deprived of Self . . . ; this play of alternation takes place every time the Witz intervenes.)[3]

> We agreed on this, that Kant discovered the "thing as it is in itself" (*Ding an sich, chose en soi*), which is according to him unknowable, on the basis of the castration complex, which is combined with anxiety over onanism and hermaphroditic complexes. The thing just as it is may thus be the thing just as Kant. . . .
> —George Groddeck, Letter to Freud, May 9, 1922

It's not only a question of a syncope described, "discoursed" [*discourue*], but rather of a syncope *of* discourse: in effect, the salutary properties of laughter can only be *more or less* understood. In order to explain it, one must invoke a relation between the body and thought about which Kant has, in truth, *nothing* to say:

> For if we assume that all our thoughts are, in addition, in a harmonious connection with some agitation in the body's organs . . . (*CJ*, 205)

(yet how can one admit this, when one is no longer Leibniz? How can one admit in general a harmony in *kant*? We have already had to confront this question. . . .)

> It is not our judging of the harmony we find in tones or in flashes of wit—this harmony, with its beauty, merely serves as a necessary

> vehicle—but the furtherance of the vital pro-
> cesses of the body, the affect that agitates the
> intestines and the diaphragm, in a word the
> feeling of health (which we cannot feel with-
> out such prompting), which constitutes the
> gratification . . . the understanding, failing
> to find what it expected, suddenly relaxes, so
> that we feel the effect of this slackening in the
> body by the vibration of the organs. . . . (*CJ*,
> 203)

The union of soul and body—the union that here gives itself
sexual airs—which is just as well the sublime union of the thought
and the unthought (of the nonrepresented)—this union which is
not one, which is not the reunion of two orders or of two substances, but which is—if it *is* indeed some thing—the *flesh* of the
philosopher—this union of the heterogeneous does not make up
the object of a knowledge.

> Now it is ridiculous to ask what sort of opin-
> ion you have about the communion of the
> soul with the body, the nature of a spirit,
> or creation in time. I have no opinion at all
> about these things. But what origin in the hu-
> man understanding these thoughts have, even
> though they go beyond its boundaries; why
> these questions are necessary and why with
> regard to the object they can be answered
> only subjectively: that *I know*. . . . (*NF*, 202)

In order to think its own laughter (which it *needs* so it can
live, so it can feel itself), thinking passes through the thought of
its nonknowing. In order to think, thinking thinks through the
thought of nothing—through the trembling of a nonrepresenta-
tion and a nonpresentation. The system syncopates itself over the
void of Darstellung—and the syncope cannot be explained, only
"acknowledged"—and consequently, somehow, *erdichtet*. Laughter
is the fictional notion (or the literary process) whereby the philos-

opher achieves self-presence.—That's why, to summarize without interruption the text of the third *Critique*, one rediscovers the *genius*, over whom Kant allows himself or finds himself constrained to laugh:

> Voltaire said that heaven has given us two things to counterbalance the many hardships in life: *hope* and *sleep*. He might have added *laughter*, if only the means for arousing it in reasonable people were as easy to come by, and if the wit or whimsical originality needed for it were not just as rare, as the talent is common for people to write, as mystical ponderers do, things that *break your head*, or to write, as geniuses do, things that *break your neck*, or to write, as sentimental novelists do (also, I suppose, sentimental moralists), things that *break your heart*. (*CJ*, 205)

The equivocation here is extreme. Between the "mystical" and the "sentimental," between the "superior" [*grand-seigneur*] and the "novelist," the genius could well be the philosopher, who would then right away make fun of and/or pride himself on calling himself a *daredevil*. But it's also a "talent that is widespread" . . . a subaltern genius? Or not exactly average?—At the same time, Logodaedalus, once more, catches himself in time here. He manages to put himself on guard without saying so, but by *making words*, by the rarest of talents, the talent of Witz and comedy. And yet, this comedy is neither demonstrable nor presentable in theory: If Logodaedalus is neither a mystic nor a novelist, nor a *genius*, since he taunts all of them, what is left? A strange and untenable collusion between a joker and a laborious metaphysician. This figure—a logodaedalus of which every element would be worth its full value—would have to raise himself above the genius himself, above his risks and his absurdities. In reality, he blacks out and disperses himself before he is barely constituted. He does not succeed in sustaining himself [*se tenir*] in discourse.

In knotting the problem of the relation between philosophy

and literature, philosophy probably allowed to escape that which, in philosophy, without elegance but not without the unsettling appeal of disgrace has not ceased to undo its pretensions—most singularly, its will to being literature, Darstellung, presentation, genre, or style.

> Kant seems to have created for himself a painful language. And just as it was painful for him to construct it, it is painful to understand. Which is probably why he often took its operation as its matter. He thought he could make ideas by only making words.
> —Joseph Joubert, *Carnets*

However, what if "operation"—the work and the calculation of the work, or the putting to work of the work, or even the making of philosophy into *a work*, its Darstellung or its Dichtung—was precisely Kant's *matter*? The materiality *itself*, so to speak, the loss of all metaphysical "matters": the Thing, Knowledge, the System—or *the material passage of philosophy to its ruin*? The imparting [*le partage*] and confusion of "philosophy" and "literature," of truth and elegance, respond (confusedly, through indecision) to the injunction: "Thou must discourse." To obey this order with a *pure* discourse makes no sense because discourse is always already a (the) *manner* of literature. But to overcome this order and replace it with another makes no sense either because this imperative constitutes philosophy as such. And in the space and history of philosophy, no one can boast of the death of meaning. This space and history are structured by the kant of philosophy: they are *limited*, most certainly, but one only ever transgresses limits by reconstituting the boundaries: for example, when one claims to go on to literature, or to poetry. By contrast, in this space and in this history, in every place, every instant, and every kant, the presentation of meaning inscribes its *undecidable* proposition. And it's perhaps by this that all discourse and all meaning endure. Meaning undecides itself.

As Maurice Blanchot, Kant's most rigorous commentator,

writes, "Philosophical discourse always gets lost at a certain point; perhaps it is even nothing but an inexorable way of losing and of losing oneself."[4] There still remains something to say [*discourir*] materially in this loss, if it is still a question of spending the inevitable, laughable profit of a cognition, an Idea, or a style; there still remains, at least, on the edge or the limit of discourse—in reality never attained, and yet always transgressed, or disturbed—there remains, therefore, the exhausting because indeterminate—and always unsettling—necessity to write, that is to say, to mark something (what? to mark perhaps means: to undecide) between philosophy and literature, between philosophy and itself. Finally, what remains written is never neither here nor there, nor even probably elsewhere.[5]

In December 1803, he became incapable of signing his name . . . from irretention of memory, he could not recollect the letters which composed his name, and when they were repeated to him, he could not represent the figure of the letters in his imagination.
—Thomas De Quincey, "Last Days of Immanuel Kant"

Appendix: Some Further Citations Regarding Kant

Jacques, remember this. Only beauty is not fleeting. Those who grasp it in the flesh are the equals of those who grasp it with the mind. Whether one embraces one's lover or the problems of the world, one has always embraced the world. . . . Come now, you love each other. Admit it. You are alone. An old wise man . . . doesn't count . . . for the living. And one in the arms of the other, with his dry hands, he pushed them, under the stars. —Léon Daudet[1]

Question: What do you think of Kant?
Answer: The nudity of the woman is wiser than the teachings of the philosopher. —Max Ernst

As if it were from yesterday the mammoth
The mastodon the first kisses
The ice ages bring nothing new
The great heat of the thirteenth in their era
Over Lisbon smoking Kant coolly hunched over . . .
—Samuel Beckett

What is *cant*, you will ask. *Cant*, says Johnson's celebrated English dictionary, is the *pretense of having morality and goodness, expressed in wailing; depressing, affected and conventional language.* —Stendhal, *Mélanges de littérature*

While Immanuel Kant was washing the windows
he recalled that yesterday's laundry

was still floating in the tub
and he put away his rag . . .
—Heidi Paraki

Now Törless had only ever heard the name of Kant uttered occasionally and then with a curious expression, as though it was the name of some sinister holy man. And Törless could only imagine that Kant had solved the problems of philosophy once and for all, and that since that time those problems had been merely a pointless occupation, just as he believed that there was no point in writing poetry after Schiller and Goethe. —Robert Musil, *The Confusions of Young Törless*

Notes

Translator's Introduction

1. To the extent that Nancy is working from and in the wake of Heidegger and all he represents in the development of French thought during the second half of the twentieth century, he certainly may be included under this rubric. However, as the polemical preamble makes clear, if by the term "French theory" one understands "the end of metaphysics" and the "end of philosophy," as a historical epoch of a one-dimensional "postmodern" free play of the signifier, or the validation of an indeterminate "interdisciplinarity"—or even the transformation of psychoanalysis into a master discourse in humanistic study—then Nancy, who always insists on the necessity of philosophizing, must be excluded from the category (ultimately, of course, the term is far too diffuse and baggy to be very useful). Indeed, it is possibly one of the interests of reading this book today to see just how the question of "French theory," which was at the center of so much polemic in the American context, was treated within France, above all within "French theory" "itself."

2. Walter Benjamin, "The Task of the Translator," trans. Harry Zohn, in *Selected Writings*, vol. 1, ed. Marcus Bullock and Michael W. Jennings (Cambridge, MA: Harvard University Press, 1996), 258.

3. Ibid., 259.

4. See Nancy's *The Speculative Remark: (One of Hegel's Bons Mots)*, trans. Céline Surprenant (Stanford, CA: Stanford University Press, 2001); and a book he cowrote with Philippe Lacoue-Labarthe, *The Literary Absolute: The Theory of Literature in German Romanticism*, trans.

Philip Barnard and Cheryl Lester (Albany: State University of New York Press, 1988).

5. See her translator's introduction, "Speaking in Water," in Jean-Luc Nancy, *The Speculative Remark: (One of Hegel's Bons Mots)*, trans. Céline Surprenant (Stanford, CA: Stanford University Press, 2001), x.

Preface

1. Antonin Artaud, *Cahiers de Rodez,* in *Oeuvres complètes*, vol. 20 (Paris: Gallimard, 1984), 450.

2. *The Correspondence of Walter Benjamin, 1910–1940*, ed. and annot. Gershom Scholem and Theodor W. Adorno; trans. Manfred R. Jacobson and Evelyn M. Jacobson (Chicago: University of Chicago Press, 1994), 97–98.

Chapter 1

1. [See note 4 below.—Trans.]

2. [Translation modified.] G. W. F. Hegel, *Lectures on the History of Philosophy,* trans. E. S. Haldane, vol. 1 (Lincoln: University of Nebraska Press, 1995), 483–84.

3. Kant was editing the *Critique of Judgment* in 1789.

4. [Originally, Nancy's *Discourse of the Syncope* was intended to have two volumes, the first of which is *Logodaedalus*. The second volume, *Kosmotheoros*, to which he refers here and on several other occasions, was never published. However, readers familiar with the broader arc of Nancy's work might well recognize the motif of the cosmological submerged underneath the notions of space, spacing, and world that figure so prominently in his later writings, especially in *The Sense of the World* and *The Creation of the World: Or Globalisation*. The term "Cosmotheoros" appears in several of Kant's posthumous notes, but derives in Nancy's view from the fact that when he reduces the program of philosophy to the critical task of accounting for the conditions of the possibility of knowledge from experience alone, he effectively brackets all cosmological accounts of the universe. In the *Critique of Pure Reason*, Kant writes:

> The concepts of reality, substance, causality, and even of necessity in existence have—apart from the use whereby they make empirical cognition of an object possible—no signification whatever that would determine any object. Hence, they can indeed be used to explain the possibility of things in the

world of sense, but not the possibility of a *world whole itself*, because the basis for explaining this world whole would have to be outside the world and hence could not be an object of possible experience. (*CPR*, 644)

To the extent that he deprives reason of the ability to know the un-conditioned, or, more importantly, to ground itself therein, Kant ruins all cosmologies that presume a Creator. He thereby clears the way for reason's autofoundation and conceives the world as something like a pure Idea unlike the other Ideas of pure reason, God and the soul, which are ideals. The world is the phenomenon of the Idea in its transcen-dental sense, that is, as neither a supersensible idea nor a given totality, but the outer limit and maximum of what reason can grasp, a bound-ary that Nancy will later describe as a finite infinite. In other words, following the question of *writing* the System, *Kosmotheoros* intended to pursue and explore the necessity that Kant's thought gives rise to—and which underlies Kant's *Opus postumum*—an account of *producing* the world.—Trans.]

5. Georges Bataille, *Erotisme* (Paris: Seuil, 1957), 306.

6. [Nancy here plays on the sense of *tenir* as both to speak and to master, or occupy, in the sense that one "holds" a city or a position. Thus a discourse that is *tenu* and *intenable* is at once spoken, mastered, and, at the same time, one that cannot be mastered because it cannot be "held" or "occupied." This opposition must also be heard alongside the one implied here between the "spoken" and the "unspeakable." See note 9 below and my Translator's Introduction.]

7. As they have also pointed out, from different perspectives: Alain Badiou, in his "Marque et manque," published in *Cahiers pour l'analyse* no. 10 (1969); and J. T. Desanti, *La philosophie silencieuse* (Paris: Seuil, 1975), 261.

8. On one side and the other, in parallel, but also by way of a chias-mus of their functions, the discourse of foundation and the discourse of operation are caught in the same transport; tendentiously or asymptoti-cally, it's a transport or excess of the same by the same. Thus begins or announces itself a transformation of the problems related to "science" that may be considerable, a transformation that is nonetheless quite for-eign to all "philosophy of science" as well as to all "epistemology"—or, to say it differently, of which epistemology has up until now provided only the most remote and palest of symptoms. However, this is not the place to consider these questions. They will have to be taken up elsewhere.

9. Allow me to lend authority to this proposition by referring to my book *The Speculative Remark: (One of Hegel's Bons Mots)*, trans. Céline Surprenant (Stanford, CA: Stanford University Press, 2001), where I sought to demonstrate how the dialectic *itself* undecides itself, or functions only by means of decisions taken elsewhere. The *Aufheben* is the upside down, decided, and even twice-decided figure of the undecidable.

10. [Here, the polarity of control/chaos implied in the previous opposition, discussed in note 5 above, is doubled, as it is above as well, with the polarity of spoken/unspoken, which I have chosen to accentuate here. The reader should keep in mind that both polarities are operating in both instances.]

11. [Nancy is here playing on the double meaning of "ça," which in French is both a pronoun meaning "that" or "it" and the Freudian "id." He is, of course, alluding to Lacan's famous pun, *ça parle*, "it/the id speaks."]

12. [Nancy notes in the epigraph to Chapter 3 that "kant" was a participle of the German *kennen*, to know. See page 22.]

13. Bataille, *Erotisme.*

Chapter 2

1. This chapter's title alludes to the famous concluding line—"Et tout le reste est literature"—of Paul Verlaine's *L'art poétique*, a quasi-polemical poem written in 1874 wherein the poet takes issue not only with nineteenth-century Romantic poetry but also with the Parnassian school then dominant in France. The term "literature" appears therein, according to a first reading at least, in a derogatory manner.

2. We shall not try to find out here what a philosophical style could be, nor what has been said about style or styles in philosophy. Such questions would exceed our competence. Thus, "style" here should be taken only in its most general acceptation, one that corresponds to philosophy's will to being a discourse, by definition, *without* style.

3. Which is not to say that this question dates from the period from which we shall pick it up. It would be more correct to say that this period dates it. But this question has probably always philosophized in philosophy, which has always probably written it into its texts. It is not for us to treat this question as such. In this regard, the sharply circumscribed study that follows here depends on both the work of Jacques Derrida

and the work that has been pursued by Philippe Lacoue-Labarthe on the relation between philosophy and literature since his "La fable: (philosophie et literature)" (*Poètique* 1 [1970]), his "Le détour" (*Poètique* 5 [1971]), all the way to his "L'Imprésentable," which was included, along with an early version of the beginning of this book, in *Poètique* 21. In the field thus marked out, we are only risking here a marginal incursion on account of Kant.

4. [Translation modified.] See Plato, *Republic*, trans. Paul Shorey, in *Plato: The Collected Dialogues*, ed. Edith Hamilton and Huntington Cairns (Princeton, NJ: Princeton University Press, 1989), 736 (501c).

5. [Translation modified.] See Friedrich Schlegel, *Philosophical Fragments*, trans. Peter Firchow (Minneapolis: University of Minnesota Press, 1991), 23.

6. [Translation modified.] See Heinrich Heine, *Religion and Philosophy in Germany*, trans. John Snodgrass (Albany: State University of New York Press, 1986), 111.

7. "I have some notion of my privileges as a writer; in a few instances I have been told, too, how getting used to my writings 'spoils' one's taste. One simply can no longer endure other books, least of all philosophical works. It is a distinction without equal to enter this noble and delicate world—one must not by any means be a German!" See Friedrich Nietzsche, *Ecce Homo*, trans. Walter Kaufmann (New York: Vintage Books, 1967), 263.

8. [Translation modified.] See Carlo Fruttero and Franco Lucentini, *Sunday Woman*, trans. William Weaver (New York: Harcourt Brace Jovanovitch, 1973).

Chapter 3

1. Friedrich Nietzsche, *The Twilight of the Idols*, trans. Richard Hollingdale (New York: Penguin Books, 1998), 67.

2. Immanuel Kant, *Nova dilucidatio* in *Theoretical Philosophy: 1755–1781*, trans. and ed. David Walford and Ralf Meerbote (Cambridge: Cambridge University Press, 1992), 5. Allow us once more to ruthlessly place alongside one another the two extremities of a history or the two poles of a crisis. Here is Bataille: "I think in the way a girl takes off her dress"; and "What accomplishes is joy, beautiful nakedness, the elegance of lively movements, luxury, too. . . . The girl degrades herself in undressing, she gives herself up, and I, too, become vile, a parched animal."

Georges Bataille, *Oeuvres complètes*, vol. 5 (Paris: Gallimard, 1973), 200 and 538.

3. Immanuel Kant, *Theoretical Philosophy: 1755–1781*, trans. and ed. David Walford and Ralf Meerbote (Cambridge: Cambridge University Press, 1992), 112.

4. Ibid.

5. Immanuel Kant, *Observations on the Feeling of the Beautiful and the Sublime*, trans. John T. Goldthwait (Berkeley: University of California Press, 1991), 56.

6. Immanuel Kant, *Metaphysical Foundations of Natural Science*, trans. Michael Friedman, in *Theoretical Philosophy After 1781*, ed. Henry Allison and Peter Heath (Cambridge: Cambridge University Press, 2002), 192.

7. *Ak*, 8:183.

8. And first of all, to the *Letters on the Kantian Philosophy*, which contain many remarks on the theme. It would be fastidious to enumerate the full list, but to this end, we shall refer to some of the most significant letters further on.—One should also mention Kant's repeated use of another genre of excuse, which concerns, one could say, the material aspect and minutiae of elegance (but doesn't elegance always have to do with the *materiality* of discourse?): printing errors, which Kant meticulously points out on several occasions. For example, at the end of the preface to the *Only Possible Argument in Support of the Demonstration of the Existence of God*, in the first preface to the *Critique of Pure Reason*, or in that of the first edition of the *Religion Within the Boundaries of Mere Reason* (in the case of which, he often blames it on the lack of time for the necessary corrections).—And, in order to complete the picture of what obviously functions in the manner of an obsession with him, the specific interest Kant (who lived for a long time in the house of a bookseller) takes in the legal and material issues regarding the publication of books. Cf. *What Is a Book?* In the chapter on the "Doctrine of Right" in the *Metaphysics of Morals, On the Wrongfulness of Unauthorized Publication of Books*, 1785, and *On Turning Out Books*, 1798, along with the postface to the *Conflict of the Faculties*, to which we shall have to return briefly later in this book, and perhaps for a longer spell, in the second volume (*Kosmotheoros*).

9. Immanuel Kant, *Correspondance*, trans. and ed. Arnulf Zweig (Cambridge: Cambridge University Press, 1999), 202.

10. Cf. §6 and after.

11. We know that it is a matter of considerable revisions to certain passages, and above all those in which it is a question of the deduction

of concepts, where, according to Heidegger, the role of the imagination recedes—and with it, Kant retreats from the most audacious advances of his own thought. This is not irrelevant to the question we are examining here, but we shall have to analyze it in the second volume, *Kosmotheoros*.

12. This preface prefaces, moreover—or perhaps definitively—an entire and very specific program for the presentation of the *book of philosophy* after Kant, insofar as it will be conceived precisely as both a philosophical literature and (or) as philosophy, thus without literature. We had already pointed out one aspect of this program (cf. *The Speculative Remark: [One of Hegel's Bons Mots],* note 10), with the help of this, along with other texts, by Kant. Let us mark here, in circling back to it, the theme of the *incompletion* of the philosophical work such as one will find it within Hegel himself: "In regards to Platonic exposition, anyone who labors at presenting anew an independent structure of philosophical science may be reminded of the story that Plato revised his *Republic* seven times over. The recollection of this, the comparison, insofar as one may seem to be implied in it, should only urge one all the more to wish that, for a work which, belonging to the modern world, is confronted by a more profound principle, a more difficult subject matter, and a material richer in compass, leisure had been afforded to revise it seven and seventy times." See the preface to the 1831 edition of Hegel's *Science of Logic,* trans. A. V. Miller (Atlantic Highlands, NJ: Humanities Press, 1989; c. 1969), 42. [Translation modified.] Or still, and in a different way, in Feuerbach: "It is true that the subject of my work is of universal human interest; moreover, its fundamental ideas, though not in the form in which they are here expressed, or in which they could be expressed under existing circumstances, will one day become the common property of mankind: for nothing is opposed to them in the present day but empty, powerless illusions and prejudices in contradiction with the true nature of man. But in considering this subject in the first instance, I was under the necessity of treating it as a matter of science, of philosophy, and in rectifying the aberrations of Religion, Theology, and Speculation, I was naturally obliged to use their expressions. . . . " See Ludwig Feuerbach, *Essence of Christianity,* trans. George Eliot (New York: Harper & Row, 1957), xliii. One could also read the long story of the hesitations and reworkings by Husserl of his *Logical Investigations* in their second preface (once again, it's a question of the second—the problem may still take the form of the *republication* of the philosophical book). Etc.

13. And also in the *Discipline of Pure Reason*, II: " . . . but that terrain [of pure theology and psychology] can bear no combatant in his full armor and equipped with weapons that we need fear" (*CPR*, 691).

14. To be precise, one should add the following: a supplement of presentation, elegance can also be a supplementary property, that is, at once auxiliary and superfluous. In the *Critique of Judgment*, §62 says of mathematical demonstration that one could call it "beautiful, since such a demonstration makes understanding and imagination, the powers of concepts and of their a priori exhibition, respectively, feel invigorated. . . . (That [invigoration of understanding and imagination], when it is combined with the precision that reason introduces, is called the demonstration's elegance)" (*CJ*, 244). Discourse thus needs what is added to presentation as if with grace, and by a singular "invigorating a priori" [modified]. The remedy of the first is the wealth or the grace of the second. The *same* elegance is thus double, and its duplicity lies in its two roles: insofar as it is elegance of *presentation*, it is at the same time its glory *and* a kind of necessary excess—*as if in order to present one always needed a little bit more than simple presentation.* Insofar as it is the elegance of exposition, it simultaneously corresponds to a "lucid Darstellung," and thus to the pure and simple logical clarity of discourse, *and* to an ornamentation (that is "popular," we shall speak of this later) or a necessary pleasure; *as if the well-turned style had to bring the exposition closer to being the most direct presentation.* In between these two "as ifs," one can see a proposition begin to sketch itself that is common to both of them: the "well-turned" should be the equivalent of an exposition "without detour." The whole question of philosophical elegance would thus be to know what "well-turned" means, a question that is perhaps as inadmissible for philosophy as it is unavoidable. . . . The entire problematic of *Logodaedalus* is thus contained in the following: *How does one get around this question* [contourner], *how does one divert it* [détourner], *how does one get lost in its turns and returns* [tours et retours]?

15. [Nancy cites Baudelaire's translation of De Quincey, which is substantially different from the original. My translation is thus modified to give the reader some sense of Baudelaire's version.]

16. The *Anthropology* and the third *Critique* in particular. See also the beginnings of the *Groundwork*. In fact, one would have to show that this bastard proposition, a chiasmus of logic and anthropology, paradoxically *guarantees*, at least for one part, the complex unity of projects and programs on which critique operates in general, from gnoseology to aesthet-

ics. This is not without its consequences for what one will be able to say about the Kantian *system*.

17. Cf. Otto Schöndorffer, *Der elegante Magister*, in *Reichl's Philosophischer Almanach* (Darmstadt: n.p., 1924). See also the materials gathered by G. Lehman in *Kants Lebenkrise* (*La crise dans la vie de Kant*), in *Beïtrage zur Geschichte und Interpretation der Philosophie Kants* (Berlin: n.p., 1969), which explores the question of a personal, moral, and emotional crisis toward the end of the "precritical" period—and to which one would then have to be able to pose the question not of the "relation between the life and the work," but rather of something that one could provisionally call the *biographical crisis*, in giving to "biography" something of the sense, if it is a sense, that the word carries in subtitle in Roger Laporte's *Fugue: Biographie* and *Fugue: Supplément* (Paris: Gallimard, 1970 and 1973). Let us add, concerning biography, that Kant refused to have his published in his lifetime. See the *Letters*, in *Ak*, 11:540; the same was true for his correspondence. See *Ak*, 10:167 and 267. One should not forget that the epigraph of the second edition of the *Critique of Pure Reason*, taken from Bacon, begins as follows: "De nobis ipsis silemus. . . ."

18. *Ak*, 16:3,476. "Big book: big evil" is a maxim taken from Callimachus by Addison. (The note that follows is no. 3,477.)

19. That is, from Bacon to Lambert by way of Leibniz and Baumgarten, a kind of generalized exchange of themes and questions that are *divided after the fact and for us* into rhetoric, aesthetics, literary, or logical: the *inventio*, the calculus of probability, the analogy of the plausible, modeling, the algebra of the unknown, teleological imagination, the happiness of inspiration, the Witz, the combinatorial, the art of systems, etc. In short, what one might call a generalized ingenuity, in all the extension and comprehension of the term, and which it would be necessary to analyze as the relief map and the posterity of the Cartesian couple of evidence and deduction.

20. These motifs will be repeated throughout the text, which decidedly rehashes the reception given to the first *Critique*; thus, in §4, where it will be said that if Hume had arrived at Kant's reflections, he would have "infinitely profited, thanks to his style, which is of an inimitable beauty"—(however, Kant here repeats a problem the preliminary state of which is evident in Hume himself, for example in the beginning of the *Enquiry*, in the following form: "The anatomist presents to the eye the most hideous and disagreeable objects; but his science is useful to

the painter in delineating even a Venus or an Helen." David Hume, *Enquiries Concerning Human Understanding and Concerning the Principles of Morals*, ed. L. A. Selby-Bigge and P. H. Nidditch [Oxford: Clarendon Press, 1975], 10.)

21. [Translation modified.] Denis Diderot, *Ruines et Paysages: Salon de 1767* (Paris: Hermann, 1995), 216.

22. The image goes back in Kant's work to at least the *M. Immanuel Kant's Announcement of the Programme of his Lectures for the Winter Semester 1765–1766* (1765) in *Theoretical Philosophy, 1755–1770*.

Chapter 4

1. [Queneau is punning here: "Kant, dira-t-on" sounds likes the French expression "*Qu'en dira-t-on*," which means literally "what would people say" and designates the kind of rumor and slander that proverbially circulates in a small town.]

2. For the origins of the expression and the role of this "current" or this *genre* of philosophy, one can consult L. Braun, *Histoire de l'histoire de la philosophie* (Paris: Orphuys, 1973), 160.—Allow us to note that the problem of "popularity" takes up a number of notes in Kant's *Nachlass*—as well as numerous passages in his letters: for example, see, among others, the complicated and reserved congratulations Kant addresses to Marcus Herz for the popularity of his course in 1779 (*Ak*, 10:145).

3. Immanuel Kant, *On History*, trans. Lewis White Beck, Robert E. Anchor, and Emil L. Fackenheim (New York: Macmillan, 1988), 27–28.

4. [Nancy is referring, of course, to Descartes' *Metaphysical Meditations* and to Spinoza's *Ethics*.]

5. One should also, in order to bring these two quotes together, cite the note on pg. 187 in *Religion Within the Boundaries of Mere Reason*, which reserves for the Bible the *scientific* interest of being able to return to our origins "with some appearance of authenticity."

6. *Wortklauber*: someone who twists words, or who quibbles over them, and consequently, the one who fabricates them, by an excessive concern with finding the right or the striking word. The *Klauberei* is a triage operation carried out with an excessive and exhausting minutiae, a *cleavage* (the root is the same) the relentlessness of which ends up with artificial products. We shall see the logodaedalus pass through all these values, and we shall add a few of our own.

7. *Sound* reason, or *sound* understanding—expressions that Kant bor-

rows from popular philosophy—constitute a gnoseology and a therapy to trace alongside Kantian pathology and psychiatry, and which are consistently related to all the themes that we are following here. The relationship between presentation and health and the worries that are common to both will be more obviously evident in Chapter 4 of this study.

8. See the *Groundwork of the Metaphysics of Morals*, §1: "Transition from common rational to philosophic moral cognition"—a transition that consists, as everyone knows, in what *common* reason philosophizes *of itself.* See also the end of this section (*GW*, 59–60).

9. See also §6 in Kant's *Anthropology from a Pragmatic Point of View*, where "true popularity" marks itself again negatively: "However, the art, or rather the facility, of speaking in a sociable *tone* and in general of appearing fashionable is falsely named *popularity*—particularly when it concerns science. It should rather be called polished superficiality, because it frequently cloaks the paltriness of a limited mind" (*A*, 28).

10. *Briefwechsel zwischen Schiller und Körner: Von 1784 bis zum Tode Schillers*, vol. 3 (Stuttgart: J. G. Cotta, 1826), 51.

11. If not because of the "radical evil inherent in human nature" the origin of which remains "incomprehensible." Moreover, "Scriptures express this incomprehensibility in a historical narrative, which adds a closer determination of the depravity of our species by projecting evil at the beginning of the world, not however, within the human being, but in a *spirit* of an originally more sublime destiny" (*R*, 88–89). The story of Satan would only explain the necessity of correcting the popular by the scholastic. (That Satan had been "sublime"—this is the Luciferian question—we shall perhaps have the opportunity to speak again of this.)

12. *Ak,* 16:1,930.

13. *Ak,* 16:3,403.

14. One might think that we are passing too lightly over "but only in critique." What then is "critique"? What is *critique*? We shall pose this question further on. However, it is clear that everything turns around this question. Except if one considers the fact that it does not easily allow itself to be taken as a *center*, or confronted head on, since it is disguised by Kant's text.

15. [The term "automonstration" is an etymological play on the Old French form of *montrer*, "to show," *monstrer*, before the modern French dropped the "s." In other words, Nancy is here recalling the syncope that led to the modern form of "montrer" and that is still recalled in "demonstration" (in French as in English).]

16. See also the "Doctrine of Right" in the *Metaphysics of Morals*, where Kant writes, "Like the wooden head in Phaedrus's fable, a merely empirical doctrine of right is a head that may be beautiful but unfortunately has no brain" (*MM*, 66).

17. [On the notion of the Witz and its role in Nancy's thought, one should refer to both *The Speculative Remark: (One of Hegel's Bon Mots)*, trans. Céline Surprenant (Stanford, CA: Stanford University Press, 2001); and Philippe Lacoue-Labarthe to Jean-Luc Nancy, *The Literary Absolute: The Theory of Literature in German Romanticism*, trans. Philip Barnard and Cheryl Lester (Albany: State University of New York Press, 1988).]

18. [Translation modified.] Along with the Witz and the bon mot, as one might expect, is suspect the ambiguity of words in general. It cannot be a question in Kant—at least so it seems—of any *speculation* of language or on language. Kant's language hopelessly seeks the splitting of meanings by way of exactness, just as Hegel hopelessly seeks the sublation of meanings in the totality. And it all happens as if Hegel, when he *thinks* the happiness of the philosopher who discovers in language the word with the double meaning of speculation (*Aufheben*) were responding word for word to this text by Kant: " . . . the expressions *boni* and *mali* contain an ambiguity, owing to the poverty of the language, by which they are capable of a double sense and thus unavoidably involve practical laws in ambiguities, and the philosophy which, in using them, becomes aware of the difference of concepts in the same word but can still find no special expressions for them is forced into subtle distinctions about which there is subsequently no agreement inasmuch as the difference cannot be directly indicated by any suitable expression."

"The German language has the good fortune to possess expressions that do not allow this difference to be overlooked. For that which the Latins denominate with a single word, *bonum*, it has two very different concepts and equally different expressions as well: for *bonum* it has *das Gute* and *das Wohl*, for *malum* it has *das Böse* and *das Übel* (or *Weh*). . . . " See the *CprR*, 187–88.—On the relation to Hegel's text, it's useless to add anything. But with regard to Kant himself, we shall point out that this remark concerns the difference between the *good* (*Gute*) and the *agreeable* (*Wohl*), which is thus the nonmoral good—and that elegance, the bon mot or the flower are agreeable.

19. [Translation modified.] *The Educational Theory of Immanuel Kant*, trans. and ed. Edward Franklin Buchner (Philadelphia, PA: J. B. Lippincott, 1904), 170–71.

20. Immanuel Kant, Letter to Christian Gottfried Schütz, June 25, 1787. It is nevertheless necessary to point out that German is not yet a language that is written much in this period, nor very much read as a language of learning (cf. the long note by Thomas De Quincey on this question, despite its exaggeration). Kant's language itself abounds in archaisms and multiple borrowings, as much from dialects as from the old language of the chancellery as in idiomatic spelling, morphology, and syntax. The rectification and modernization of the language poses delicate problems even to Kant's editors to the extent that, as Ernst Cassirer had already pointed out, one risks thereby changing its content (see the afterword by W. Weischedel to his edition [Frankfurt, 1964]. Kant's problem is also one of a language and a people—which perhaps means that the double problem, on the one hand of philosophy and its literature, and on the other of a people and its language, which Romanticism will inherit and transform into the double problematic—metaphysical and political—of origin, authenticity, and unity, will have been entirely determined by a philosophical (in)decision.

21. Like logic since Aristotle, according to the first *Critique*, art stopped somewhere in history. But Kant does not say where.

22. It's not without interest to remark that the editions hesitate between "entirely given," "simply given," and just "given."

23. That is to say—must we repeat it?—that *something is repeated*, and notably from Plato—though without a doubt, and to say it too quickly, this repetition is "in reverse." Kant inherits a *genre* of philosophical discourse that as such succeeded Plato's. Similarly, it is worth adding, though it can delay us here, Kant is the inheritor of a certain *flesh* of philosophy. In his time, and only then, the philosopher definitively enters the university in order to make presentations and to expose himself in a court and from atop a rostrum.

24. [That is to say, the famous sentence beginning the conclusion of the *Critique of Practical Reason* where Kant writes, "Two things fill the mind with ever new and increasing admiration and reverence the more often and the more steadily one reflects upon them: the starry sky above me and the moral law within me" (*CprR*, 269).]

25. Friedrich Nietzsche, *Twilight of the Idols / The Anti-Christ*, trans. R. J. Hollingdale (New York: Penguin, 1968), 167.

26. See the *Critique of Pure Reason*, "The Postulates of Empirical Thought as Such," 283–302. See also §III and IV of the Introduction to Transcendental Logic.

27. Immanuel Kant, *Observations on the Feelings of the Beautiful and the Sublime*, trans. John T. Goldthwait (Berkeley: University of California Press, 1991), 46.

28. *Ak,* 16:1,658.

29. Friedrich Schiller, *Briefe I: 1772–1795*, ed. George Kurscheidt, vol. 11, *Werke und Briefe* (Frankfurt: Deutscher Klassiker Verlag, 2002), 690.

Chapter 5

1. [Once again, here Nancy has chosen to give the word in the original German.]

2. [Nancy is pointing out that "tableau" is the French translator's choice for Bild. See *Critique de la raison pure,* trans. A. Tremasaygues and B. Pacaud (Paris: Alcan, 1920).]

3. It is because the beautiful reinvests the word with Darstellung, which had been abandoned by pure reason for mathematics; it takes a renewed interest in it, for example, as "individual exhibition." See the *Critique of Judgment*, §17.

4. A. A. Cournot, *Considérations sur la marche des idées et des événements dans les temps modernes*, ed. André Robinet (Paris: J. Vrin, 1973).

5. [Here, Nancy has chosen to use the neologism "se finitiser," which I translate alternately as "to make finite" and to "definitize" in order to better render its strangeness in the original.]

6. [This quotation is taken from a collection of unpublished writings and fragments that Nietzsche scholars often refer to as the "Philosopher's Book." Here, I've modified the translation in *Philosophy and Truth: Selections from Nietzsche's Notebooks of the Early 1870's*, ed. and trans. Daniel Breazeale (Atlantic Highlands, NJ: Humanities Press, 1979), 15.]

7. Immanuel Kant, *Metaphysical Foundations of Natural Science*, trans. Michael Friedman, in *Theoretical Philosophy After 1781,* ed. Henry Allison and Peter Heath (Cambridge: Cambridge University Press, 2002), 187. See also, for example, *CPR*, 203, one among a hundred other similar passages. One might add that in the domain of artistic creation, in opposition to *imitation*, the relation between an "exemplary creator" (that is, of a genius) to another consists in "going to the same source which the other drew from" and in only "borrowing from them a procedure." This applies to artists, but equally well to scholars and saints, which demonstrates that Dichtung is not poetry and that, literary or philosophical, it is one and the same pure *poeisis* that constitutes the author's object of desire.

8. Around 1755–1757, Kant pointed out, as an example of a work on a ridiculously minor subject, that of the philologist Heinsius called *Laus Asini* (1623) (*Ak,* 16:3,446).

9. 9th *proposition*. In reality, the opposition is far more complex and tricky because the "novel" would correspond in fact to the idea of a history of humanity that follows "definite rational ends," an apparently senseless project; nevertheless, such an idea, conceived simply as a guiding thread, would be able to provide the Darstellung of a system for such a project. The system is here, therefore, similar to a novel made rational. Doubtless, it is to this treacherous situation that it owes, in addition, the fact of being seen as being at least systematic "in general"—something which, for a system, has to be considered. However, this isn't the only place in Kant where a distinction between the architectonics and individual details of the system is at work: one can follow such a distinction through the entire first *Critique,* and even *in the definition itself of the work* as a "propaedeutic" or preliminary outline of the main features of the system (of its blueprint). However, this distinction is also one that, in the preface, functions simultaneously in two registers: that of the major work and of accomplishment and that of doctrine and its elegance. Consequently, it is related to the opposition between bitterness and pleasure.—Let us pursue this a little further. The least tortuous presentation of the *Critique of Judgment,* in the preface, leads one to see that this opposition is also at work there as well: in fact, the third *Critique* is considered to be nothing other than the completion of the first *Critique,* or to be an annex to the first two. It isn't an independent part of the system—and thus not a structural component—which without it would be incomplete. . . . Always and everywhere in Kant, in the philosopher and in the writer, the more the whole is forced by its size or by haste to neglect the details in order to complete the system, the more one detail or another endlessly imposes itself, goes missing, or disturbs it. The thought of the system worries over the last detail. Yet on this account, this very ambiguous remorse for its elegance also implies the following: "If I had to wait for my system to be finished and presentable in each of its part, it would never be published. . . . " Yet why should it be published? Kant's question and (or) claim is: "*Why do I write books (good or bad) (?)*"

10. Immanuel Kant, *Raising the Tone of Philosophy: Late Essays by Immanuel Kant, Transformative Critique by Jacques Derrida,* ed. Peter Fenves (Baltimore, MD: Johns Hopkins University Press, 1993).

11. In "On a Newly Arisen Superior Tone in Philosophy," in Kant, *Raising the Tone of Philosophy*, 71.

12. Ibid., 65–66.

13. Ibid., 72.

14. "Philosophy is the invention of prose." Jacques Derrida, *Of Grammatology*, trans. Gayatri Spivak (Baltimore, MD: Johns Hopkins University Press, 1974), 287. It would be necessary to cite here in its entirety "La Fable: philosophie et littérature" by Philippe Lacoue-Labarthe (cf. note 2 in Chapter 2, above) and to refer to his work more globally, to which, here, I propose the following accompaniment: *prose* (philosophico-literary) *is the undecidable inscription of absence and the simultaneous mixing of all styles.* However, *by the same token,* prose is as little capable of freeing itself from the metaphysical obsession of pure (mathematical) presentation as it is from the Mallarméan obsession with pure poetry: " . . . le Vers, dispensateur, ordonnateur du jeu des pages, maître du livre. Visiblement soit qu'apparaisse son intégralité, parmi les marges et du blanc; ou qu'il se dissimule, nommez-le Prose, c'est lui qui demeure quelque secrète poursuite de musique, dans la réserve du Discours." In "Quant au livre" in Stéphane Mallarmé, *Oeuvres complètes*, ed. Bertrand Marchal, vol. 2 (Paris: Gallimard, 2003), 220. Therefore, in order to determine the existence of a philosophy that is purely and simply prosaic, it is a matter of knowing if there exists somewhere a Discourse without *reserve*: assuredly, this is what Kant wants, but the manner in which he constitutes his concept of *discourse* implies with just as much certainty, we have seen, the corresponding creation of a "reserve" (as for the musical nature of this "reserve," I can refer here to what will be described fleetingly in the final section of this text regarding music in Kant).

15. See Kant, *Raising the Tone of Philosophy*, 83–100.

16. See ibid., 91 [translation modified].

17. *Literature* before the letter, if one may be allowed to say, was the elementary knowledge (of the alphabet and of simple operations, for example)—and this was true in German longer than in French. The philosophy of elements (that is, the whole of the *Critique* minus the "Doctrine of Method") constitutes, therefore, in addition to being reason's manner of being atonal, a *literature* of philosophy.—In Kant, *Literatur* always has the sense of written information about knowledge and the intellectual domain in general, and the *Literat* is a "technician of science" by way of opposition to the "savant" (cf. *The Conflict of the Faculties*, introduction).

18. [In the original French, Nancy repeats the word *reste* in order to play on its polysemy, since it can mean "everything else" but also "what remains" or is "left over." I have translated it successively in two ways in order to provide the reader a sense of these multiple meanings.]

19. And why the *Letters*—if not because Plato is a philosophical adversary of Kant with a "superior tone," who had just translated them. Why take aim, as a whole, at Plato's most "prosaic" prose? Why preserve the *dialogues*? While in the *Logic*, Kant names the method of Socratic dialogue approvingly, he says not a single word about its literary form: without a doubt, it is for him completely eclipsed by the method as such and by its theatricalization of live questioning. Thus, the theatricalization is obscured by the philosophical drama, which makes the literary seem as if it were nothing. Yet, at the same time, it's not quite so simple, since Kant also acknowledges a legitimate poetic talent in Plato, one to be distinguished from the exaltation he perceives in the *Letters*. Then why preserve a poetic origin for philosophy, which resembles at that moment the origin of the "religion of priests"? . . . Let us notice, however, that neither does Kant simply try to preserve this origin: in the first *Critique*, in the midst of honoring Plato's efforts in representing the totality of ends, he excluded from this honor "what is exaggerated in Plato's manner of expression," which was good and well that of the dialogues, of the *Republic* in particular (cf. *CPR*, 365).

20. See Molière, *Le bourgeois gentilhomme* in *Oeuvres Complètes*, ed. Georges Couton, vol. 2 (Paris: Garnier, 1971), 730.

21. Where does the Kantian *system* come to happen [*advenir*]? Or why doesn't it ever come to happen [*advenir*]? Without envisaging these questions, let us at least recall that it is over them, in large part, that philosophy started over after Kant. And let us note this as well: the logodaedalic figure of the poet-prophet-philosopher, and therefore of the system itself, will have a name in the *Opus postumum*: the name of *Zoroaster*, written several times in attempts at inventing titles. (We have pointed to it from Nietzsche's perspective, in *"La thèse de Nietzsche sur la téléologie,"* in *Niezsche aujourd'hui?* [Paris: U.G.E., 1973]), vol. 1.) But Kant's Zarathoustra does not arrive; he remains in limbo. Or, it is probably more accurate to say that Kant does not entirely manage to *present* himself as Zoroaster. *In principle*, he cannot *make up his mind* [s'y decider] on the matter.

22. A Kantian concept that we shall have to examine on its own a little later on. On the question of the *type*, of *typography*, see also Philippe

Lacoue-Labarthe, *Typography, Mimesis, Politics*, trans. Christopher Fynsk (Cambridge, MA: Harvard University Press, 1989).

23. Immanuel Kant, *Metaphysical Foundations of Natural Science,* in *Theoretical Writings After 1781*, trans. and ed. David Walford and Ralf Meerbote (Cambridge: Cambridge University Press, 1992), 188.

24. *Ak,* 16:1,911.

25. The rhetorician in question is Theodorus, whom Plato ironically describes as "the great Byzantine word-maker." Plato, *Phaedrus*, trans. R. Hackforth, in *Plato: The Collected Dialogues ed. Edith Hamilton and Huntington Cairns* (Princeton, NJ: Princeton University Press, 1989), 512 (266e).

26. Stendhal, *The Red and the Black: A Chronicle of the Nineteenth Century*, trans. Catherine Slater (Oxford: Oxford University Press, 1991), 250.

Chapter 6

1. [Nancy is referring here, once more, to his never-published *Kosmotheoros*. See my Translator's Introduction.]

2. "There exists in us the seeds of science, like in a silex (the seeds of fire); philosophers extract these through reason; poets rip them out with the imagination, and thus they burn brighter." René Descartes, *Olympiques* in *Œuvres philosophiques*, vol. 1 (Paris: Garnier, 1953), 61. This does not mean, as we can read in this text, that this divide is without problems in Descartes. We shall return to this elsewhere.

3. Historically speaking, it is often forgotten that Kant's youth belongs to an epoque in which "popular philosophy" brushes up against, as its double, innumerable attempts at (bad) "philosophical poetry," and of which, furthermore, Poetry complains, just as Philosophy complains about its popular presentations. . . . —The following lines by Gilbert (a French poet who died in 1780), for example, bear witness to this, and we shall here cite them for the pleasure of their symmetry with Kant:

> In past times, poetry in its pompous accords,
> Daring even to lend a soul to nothingness,
> Enlivened reason with its cheerful pictures,
> And concealed the harsh precepts of virtue,
> Beneath the enchanting veil of pleasant fictions . . .
> Cursed be forever the squabbling sophist
> Who is the first to say in algebraic prose:

Vain rhyme-makers, listen to my absolute commands,
To please my reason, think, and paint no more.

4. [Translation modified.] *Johann Georg Hamann's Relational Meta-criticism,* trans. Gwen Griffith Dickson (Berlin and New York: Walter de Gruyter, 1995), 523.

5. See the "Architectonic" in *CPR,* 756. More precisely, the "charm" is simultaneously external and internal to the system. If the structure of knowledge as such possesses it by itself, such and such a part of the whole, which "would not be without usefulness nor without appeal" (as the complete tableau of derivative categories), can be neglected in the *Critique* (cf. *CPR,* 95). In playing on a completion that is now in the whole, now in the part (we have already pointed to this game), Kant authorizes a permanent displacement of the function of "charm" or of "elegance" that clouds the issue. A certain *pleasure* remains the infinitely displaceable, deformable, and polymorphous invariable of Kant's systematic dislocation.

6. See the First Introduction, in *CJ,* 394–97.

7. This takes place, in fact, not accidentally, but by virtue of the principle itself of displacement, if it is possible and necessary to show that the *Anthropology* is in some sense a repetition of the system itself—of this system structurally fated to repeating itself—upon which it confers some of its features in return. Obviously, this statement must be related back to those of Heidegger on Kantian anthropology, as well as to the analyses made by, for example, G. Krüger, *Critique de la morale chez Kant,* French trans. M. Régnier (Paris: Beauchêne, 1961).

The demonstration of it is forthcoming in my *Kosmotheoros.* (Cf. Translator's Introduction.)

8. It is on the basis of these considerations that, in the examination of schematism, one would have to examine Heidegger's interpretation of the "retreat" of the imagination in Kant, since this "retreat" is, as we can see, roundabout.

9. In the whole history of the Witz, from Romanticism to the present day, the idea of a sublime or grandiose Witz was always considered according to a manner captured in the following formula: "One can only speak about a '*grandiose*' Witz *by way of a Witz.*" See André Wellek, *Witz-Lyrik-Sprache* (Bern: n.p., 1970). Or the sublime in a Witz is the grotesque.

10. See also "Architectonic," in *CPR,* 755–70; and *CJ,* §68.

11. *CJ*, §23, §26, §27, and §29.

12. See Chapter 4, note 11, above. The question of evil should be pursued for itself elsewhere alongside Jacques Lacan's "Kant with Sade," *Écrits* (Paris: Seuil, 1966). Moreover, one ought not forget that the victorious adversary of Satan—trading on his sacrifice—Christ, is the one that the holy narrative represents as being born of a virgin mother. Kant points out that the absence of sexual relation—the absence of the union of the heterogeneous, and the absence of pleasure, or even the purity of the source—is very suitable to the representation of the moral idea in a model. This suitability is so powerful that it even pushes Kant to sketch out a peculiar gesture: the attempt to establish, on this point, the *letter* (and not only the symbolic meaning) of the biblical story. He sketches, in effect, between the theses of epigenesis and preformation, a biological theory of the *Immaculate Conception*—and thus holds himself very close to the operation by which Hegel, in a speculative rather than biological register, intends to "lift the veil covering or resolve the contradiction of the dogma of the Virgin Mary." See Jacques Derrida, *Glas* (Paris: Galilée, 1974), 228. On the point of the *immaculate conception*, Kant is very close *to affirming (sacred) literature itself according to the concept*. But he all of a sudden interrupts the gesture he sketches out: "But what is the use of all this theorizing *pro* and *contra* . . . " (*R*, 119). In fact, what is it good for, if critique has indeed ahead of time rendered the conceptual determination and presentation of the phenomena of *life* impossible, if it has submitted these to the regime of reflection, analogy, and symbol, and if consequently *conception in general* (immaculate or not) *cannot be thought without blemishes* [macules]?

13. In this text, see especially the "Doctrine of Method," 261–71.

14. Immanuel Kant, *Toward Perpetual Peace* in *Practical Philosophy*, trans. and ed. Mary J. Gregor (Cambridge: Cambridge University Press, 1996), 336. The stakes are those of a—if not *the*—system, "but achievement is difficult because one cannot expect to reach the goal by the free agreement of 'individuals,' but only by a progressive organization of citizens of the earth into and toward the species as a system that is cosmopolitically united" (*A*, 238). However, *the* system is at the very least necessarily the system of all the systems that it controls. As for the political consequences of this delimitation, these will be examined in my *Kosmotheoros*.

15. Kant, *Toward Perpetual Peace*, 336.

16. Immanuel Kant, *On History*, trans. Lewis White Beck, Robert E. Anchor, and Emil L. Fackenheim (New York: Macmillan, 1988), 45.

17. The word logodaedalie appears in Kant's *Nachlass* (*Ak,* 16:3,417) written in the margin of a text by Meier on the "grocery store of words," wherein one gives the word for the thing. On what follows regarding Kant's labyrinth, let us remark that Denis Hollier has permitted us to see after the fact that this labyrinth is already largely caught in the structure *of the* labyrinth, the one into which Hollier disappears following Bataille: "The labyrinth . . . does not have a transcendence that would permit one to explore it. Wanting to explore the labyrinth only confirms this further: there is no getting around it." Denis Hollier, *Against Architecture: The Writings of George Bataille*, trans. Betsy Wing (Cambridge, MA: MIT Press, 1989), 58.

18. On the word daidalos, see Françoise Frontisi-Ducroux, *Dèdale:*

19. *CPR,* 311.

20. *Ak,* 16:1,651.

21. *Ak,* 16:1,652.

22. [Translation modified.] *Johann Georg Hamann's Relational Metacriticism,* 523.

23. [M. Homais is the tedious village pharmacist in Gustave Flaubert's *Madame Bovary*.]

24. [Translation modified.] *The Captive,* in *Remembrance of Things Past,* trans. C. K. Scott Moncrieff, Terence Kilmartin, and Andreas Mayor, vol. 3 (New York: Vintage Books, 1982), 284. One can also revisit the figure of Verdurin, the one who "renounced writing." . . .

25. See in French, Kant's *Feuilles détachées* on the *Progrès de la métaphysique,* trans. Guillermit (Paris: Vrin, 1968), 110.

26. Karel Čapek, *War with the Newts,* trans. Ewald Osers (New Jersey: Catbird Press, 1990), 197.

27. See the 5th fascicle, sheet 4 (*Ak* 21:524) in Immanuel Kant, *Opus postumum,* ed. Eckart Förster and Michael Rosen (Cambridge: Cambridge University Press, 1995), 36.

28. Jorge-Luis Borges, *Discussion,* trans. C. Staub (Paris: Gallimard, 1966), 21.

29. Ibid., 24.

30. [Nancy is referring here to the title of Gérard Granel's *L'Équivoque ontologique de la pensée kantienne,* mentioned in note 12 in the Preamble, above.]

Chapter 7

1. [The expression used by Nancy here, "tel qu'en lui-même," is a reference to Stéphane Mallarmé's poem, *Le Tombeau d'Edgar Poe*, which begins with this clause.]

2. See the *Anthropology*, §79. An entire problematic of sneezing—which unblocks the obstructed canals of the head just as defecation unblocks the stomach (which brings us back to the cataract [*catharre*] and/or the constipation of hypochondria)—itself related to an analysis of the *nosei,* of the *nasal mucus,* and of disgust unfolds in the *Anthropology* and in the correspondence. It is also known, moreover, that sneezing has always been a sacred phenomenon—expulsion of demons, or syncope of the soul itself—and that Antiquity claimed that Socrates' demon manifested itself by a sneeze (cf. Plutarch, *"On the Sign of Socrates"* [*De genio socratis*] in the *Moralia*).

3. However, we ought not forget that "in anthropology the characteristic features of the *female* sex, more than those of the male sex, are a topic of study for the philosopher" (*A*, 204). But shouldn't the philosopher be *virile*?

4. Maurice Blanchot, "Le Discours philosophique," in *Arc* 46 (1990).

5. This is because at least the mark has its place: as we have seen, it's the very place of the system, or of the schema. In this place, another character—or the same? or his double?—confronts Logodaedalus. He will present himself under the name of Kosmotheoros.

Appendix

1. Léon Daudet was a pamphleteer of the most brutally reactionary and anti-Semitic French extreme right of the 1920s and 1930s. Furthermore, one finds several allusions to the propagation of the race in the story in question: the couple is composed of a young man whose origins are simultaneously Jewish, Spanish, and Scandinavian, whereas the young woman is pure German. . . . The embrace at the end of the text, therefore, is not alien to a certain eugenics that is never lacking in the sense of a contribution made by "new" bloods. . . . It is thus not without scruples that I include this citation. But it is necessary to recognize that it gives to the figure of Kant a particularly singular relief.—J.-L. Nancy.

MERIDIAN

Crossing Aesthetics

Giorgio Agamben, *The Time that Remains: A Commentary on the Letter to the Romans*

Jean-Luc Nancy, *Multiple Arts: The Muses II*

Alain Badiou, *Handbook of Inaesthetics*

Jacques Derrida, *Eyes of the University: Right to Philosophy 2*

Maurice Blanchot, *Lautréamont and Sade*

Giorgio Agamben, *The Open: Man and Animal*

Jean Genet, *The Declared Enemy*

Shosana Felman, *Writing and Madness: (Literature/Philosophy/Psychoanalysis)*

Jean Genet, *Fragments of the Artwork*

Shoshana Felman, *The Scandal of the Speaking Body: Don Juan with J. L. Austin, or Seduction in Two Languages*

Peter Szondi, *Celan Studies*

Neil Hertz, *George Eliot's Pulse*

Maurice Blanchot, *The Book to Come*

Susannah Young-ah Gottlieb, *Regions of Sorrow: Anxiety and Messianism in Hannah Arendt and W. H. Auden*

Jacques Derrida, *Without Alibi*, edited by Peggy Kamuf

Cornelius Castoriadis, *On Plato's 'Statesman'*

Jacques Derrida, *Who's Afraid of Philosophy? Right to Philosophy 1*

Peter Szondi, *An Essay on the Tragic*

Peter Fenves, *Arresting Language: From Leibniz to Benjamin*

Jill Robbins, ed. *Is It Righteous to Be?: Interviews with Emmanuel Levinas*

Louis Marin, *Of Representation*

Daniel Payot, *The Architect and the Philosopher*

J. Hillis Miller, *Speech Acts in Literature*

Maurice Blanchot, *Faux pas*

Jean-Luc Nancy, *Being Singular Plural*

Maurice Blanchot / Jacques Derrida, *The Instant of My Death / Demeure: Fiction and Testimony*

Niklas Luhmann, *Art as a Social System*

Emmanual Levinas, *God, Death, and Time*

Ernst Bloch, *The Spirit of Utopia*

Giorgio Agamben, *Potentialities: Collected Essays in Philosophy*

Ellen S. Burt, *Poetry's Appeal: French Nineteenth-Century Lyric and the Political Space*

Jacques Derrida, *Adieu to Emmanuel Levinas*

Werner Hamacher, *Premises: Essays on Philosophy and Literature from Kant to Celan*

Aris Fioretos, *The Gray Book*

Deborah Esch, *In the Event: Reading Journalism, Reading Theory*

Winfried Menninghaus, *In Praise of Nonsense: Kant and Bluebeard*

Giorgio Agamben, *The Man Without Content*

Giorgio Agamben, *The End of the Poem: Studies in Poetics*

Theodor W. Adorno, *Sound Figures*

Louis Marin, *Sublime Poussin*

Philippe Lacoue-Labarthe, *Poetry as Experience*

Ernst Bloch, *Literary Essays*